Mediterranean Diet Cookbook for Beginners 2019

Start living the Mediterranean lifestyle to Lose weight, Balance Hormones and reinvent your Life for a New and Improved You

Robert Mancine

Table of Contents

Chapter 1: Understanding the Mediterranean Diet

The History of Mediterranean Diet

The origin of the Mediterranean diet is involved around the area along the Mediterranean Sea. These areas are also known for the initiators for the origins of the culture of the world. The eating habits of the inhabitants of these areas have developed thousands of years ago. The versatility of dietary habits can be seen in parts of Europe including Spain, Greece, Southern France, Italy, and Portugal. The Mediterranean diet can also be seen being followed in the northern parts of Africa like Tunisia and Morocco. The Mediterranean diet is also being followed by the Middle Eastern countries like Syria and Lebanon as well as by Balkan states and Turkey. The diet is too much popular because the region produces fresh veggies and fruits around the year and is consumed by people frequently. The main produce of the area includes nuts, olive oil, legumes, bread, wine and an abundant supply of fish from the Mediterranean Sea itself. Meal prepping and sharing it with others is a cultural root of the Mediterranean region and the cuisine is popular across the globe for its rich and delicious taste and flavor.

What is the Mediterranean Diet?

The Mediterranean diet is based upon the cuisines and culture of the Mediterranean region. Numerous scientific and medical studies have argued and proven that the Mediterranean diet is very healthy and is a perfect diet plan for avoiding various chronic diseases like cancer, cardiac complications and also for boosting life expectancy.
Back in the 1950s, the medical researchers had started drawing connections between diet and cardiac complications. Dr. Ancel Keys performed a study on various diets in accordance with the principles of epidemiology. The study is known as "Seven Countries Study" and has been declared the most authentic epidemiological studies ever conducted. The study involved around 13,000 male individuals from the US, Japan, Serbia, Finland, the Netherlands, and Croatia and was performed over a decade. The study was concluded on the fact that the people from the Mediterranean region had a smaller risk of getting a chronic disease related to heart an enjoyed healthier lifestyle as compared to the rest of the world. The study also argued that the mortality rate of the Mediterranean region was

comparatively low from the rest of the globe too i.e. Greek men aged between 50 to 54 had 90% lower risk of having a cardiac issue as compared to the same age group from the US.

The study also showed that the Mediterranean diet is rich in fat content has 40% of its calories subjected to its high fat. The Mediterranean diet is very different in its fat intake from the rest of the diets. Mediterranean cuisine involves higher content of unsaturated fat like olive oil and lower content of saturated fats. Saturated fats are mainly present in dairy products and meat apart from their slight presence in a few nuts, avocados and certain vegetable oils. The saturated fats are utilized by the body to make cholesterol and this has been proven various times that cardiovascular issues are strongly linked with higher cholesterol levels.

There are many scientific types of research that have further backed the work of Dr. Ancle Keys about the healthy lifestyle of the Mediterranean people. An analysis issued by the WHO in 1990 argued that Europe Mediterranean countries like Italy, Greece, France, and Spain have a lower risk of heart complications, higher life expectancy and lower risk of cancer from the rest of Europe. The analysis proved critical as these countries have high smoking populations and aren't having any properly conducted exercise programs like the American society. This indicates that this healthy lifestyle has some other factors involved. The factor of genetic variations has also been discarded by scientists because those Mediterranean who move out to other countries and get off from the Mediterranean diet also lose the health advantages the diet offered. These studies all ponder the fact that both lifestyle and diet are critically important factors. In 1994, a French study argued that people following the Mediterranean diet are less prone to have cardiac diseases and deaths as compared to other diet followers.

The Mediterranean diet came into the limelight when the head of Nutrition Department of the Harvard University, Dr. Walter Willet recommended it to various people. Low-fat oriented diets were already being prescribed for heart issues. Mediterranean groups involved in his studies had a high-fat oriented diet which has its main fat content from olive oil. His studies argued that the risk of heart-related complications and diseases can be lowered by increasing the intake of a type of dietary fat i.e. the mono-saturated fat, which is present mostly in olive oils. This argument of Dr. Walter was completely opposite to the generally applied nutritional preferences and recommendations of eliminating all kind of fat content from diet plans to avoid heart-related problems. Studies have concluded that unsaturated fats have been credited with a high amount of HDL cholesterol which is also referred to as "the good" cholesterol. The reason for HDL cholesterol being credited as a friend for the body is that protects the body from cardiovascular complications. Dr. Willet also drew the links between meat intake with cancer and cardiovascular diseases.

Dr. Willet and the WHO along with various other researchers joined hands in 1994 and constructed the Mediterranean Food Pyramid. The Mediterranean Food Pyramid involves food from various categories and its intake amount per day to perfectly follow the Mediterranean diet plan. These researchers argue that their food groups are far more beneficial in health status as compared to the food groups designed by the USDA (United States Department of Agriculture). The USDA has listed a higher content of daily meat and dairy servings. The Mediterranean diet specialists claim that these recommendations are politically motivated and have nothing to do with dietary science at all.

Description of the Mediterranean Diet

The Mediterranean diet plan has various specific characteristics which make it different from other diet plans. These include the following:

- The major portion of the diet plan is derived from various plant related sources like bread, rice, fruits, legumes (lentils and beans), whole grains, pasta, couscous and bulgur (from wheat), potatoes, polenta (from corn), nuts and seeds.
- The leading source of fat in the diet is olive oil and is used as the main cooking oil too. It is used in abundance and approximately 35% of the calories are because of the fats. The important thing to understand is that saturated fats are only credited with 8% of the total calories only and is even lesser than this in some cases, which means that the consumption of dairy products and meat is limited.
- Veggies and fruits intake are high in numbers. Both veggies and fruits are unprocessed, locally produced, fresh and eaten in season.
- Dairy intake is limited in the Mediterranean diet plan. Dairy is consumed mostly in the form of yogurt and cheese with their amounts being 1 cup of yogurt and 1 oz. of cheese.
- Eggs are consumed around four eggs per week.

- Poultry and fish are allowed only one to three times a week. This means that it should be lower than 1 lb. per week collectively, and fish should be preferred over poultry.
- Red meat is also consumed in a limited amount i.e. once in a month while its quantity should be less than a pound in a single month.
- Honey is the main sweetening source in the Mediterranean diet. Sweet intake is also limited in this diet plan and is allowed for consumption a few times every week.
- Wine intake is moderated in nature and is allowed 1-2 glasses every day.

Benefits of the Mediterranean Diet

As explained above, the Mediterranean diet has various health benefits for its followers if it's followed consistently. Some of the most important ones are as follows:

- Preserve Memory
  The Mediterranean diet is proven to be very beneficial in preserving your memory and preventing cognitive declines. The reason is that the Mediterranean diet is high in its healthy fat content which is super beneficial for stimulating the human brain power as well as avoiding or lowering the risk of cognitive decline and dementia. A study claims constantly following the Mediterranean diet will reduce the risk of cognitive declines by around 40 percent.
- Lower Risk of Cardiovascular Complications
  The Mediterranean diet has a strong positive effect on heart-related risk factors like triglycerides, high BP and cholesterol. This is why it reduces the risk of having cardiovascular diseases like strokes, myocardial infarction (commonly known as heart attack) and coronary heart disease etc.
- Bone Strengthening
  Olive oil is used in abundance in the Mediterranean diet. Olive oil is credited with preserving and increasing bone density by incrementing the maturity and proliferation of the bone cells. The diet patterns of the Mediterranean diet are also credited with avoiding osteoporosis.
- Blood Sugar Controlling

The Mediterranean diet has been proven to control body blood sugar and diabetes. It is proven by a study that it can also reverse type-2 diabetes. It is also claimed that it can improve heart-related risks and blood sugar control in individuals already having it. The Mediterranean diet followers when observed showed, improved blood sugar, improved weight loss, lower urge to get medical treatment as compared to those having a low-fat diet plan.

- Anti-Depression

The Mediterranean diet has also been credited as an anti-depressant. A study conducted in 2013 showed that those who follow the Mediterranean diet plan has approximately 98.6% reduced risk of prone to depression than those who follow other diet plans.

- Prevents Cancer

The Mediterranean diet has been credited with anticancer properties. A study shows that those who follow the Mediterranean diet has a 13% reduced risk of having terminal cancer than those who don't follow the diet. The various cancers which can be prevented by following the Mediterranean diet include neck cancer, liver cancer, breast cancer, prostate cancer, head cancer, colorectal cancer, and gastric cancer.

Chapter 2: Starting the Mediterranean Diet

Planning the Mediterranean Diet

Although you can find numerous cookbook and recipe pamphlets for starting a Mediterranean diet, we are going to explain the basic steps which lead toward the Mediterranean diet. These include:

- The first step involves eliminating all kinds of oils, margarine, and butter by replacing it with olive oil.
- Always consume meats with salads and bread.
- American followers can visit farmer markets or places selling organic produce to grab themselves fresh veggies and fruits.
- Replace meat by legumes, whole grains and other foods for various meals.
- Always have cheese or yogurt instead of milk.
- Various other factors include having workout sessions to wade-off stress.
- The largest meal i.e. the lunch should be followed with a siesta.

Precautions

- Don't consume wine if you are having any health complications.
- Only use olive oil in abundance when it is the sole oil in your food, not as additional oil.
- Lower fat intake from dairy products, hydrogenated cooking oils, and other sources.

The top 10 tips to Success

The Mediterranean diet has been credited with a lot of health benefits which can be easily gained by simple tricks. The following tips and tricks are going to ensure you're perfectly following up on the Mediterranean diet. These include:

1. Doubling or Tripling your Veggies
   An increased number of veggies is always beneficial for your health. There are numerous researches which prove that any plant-heavy diet plan has far better health benefits than any other diet plan. According to a study, people who

consume 7 or above servings of veggies and fruits have a comparatively lower risk of cardiovascular diseases and cancer. As per the findings of another study, 10 or above servings of fruits and veggies will reduce the risk of strokes and avoid 7.8 million premature deaths.

2. Start loving legumes

Legumes are the richest protein resource included in the Mediterranean diet and they are also credited as the perfect dietary fiber resource available. A single cup of navy beans has more dietary fiber than 7 slices of bread (whole-wheat) and more protein than 2 eggs. Eat more of them.

3. Consume enough Seafood and Fish

Seafood and fishes are high in proteins, vitamin B & D, selenium and are also supported by a study that explains how consumption of 2 oz. of fish can lower the risk of death by 12 %. You should preferably consume fatty fishes.

4. Start using Olive oil

The first step for a successful Mediterranean diet is to eliminate all kinds of oils, margarine, and butter by replacing it with olive oil. There are beneficial mono-saturated fats in olive oil which produce HDL cholesterol. HDL cholesterol is credited with preventing heart issues.

5. Use fruits as desserts

Fruits are low in fat, high in fiber and also perfect antioxidants. Consuming whole-fruits can lower your risk of diabetes. For example, pears and apples are credited with lowering the risk of having heart strokes. You can use fruits as desserts or even snack them between meals.

6. Garnish using Diary

Allowed dairy products for the Mediterranean diet can be used in small amounts for garnishing. Dairy has been credited with a lower risk of heart diseases, diabetes, obesity, and metabolic syndrome.

7. Increase seasonings

The Mediterranean diet is very dependent on herbs and seasonings instead of salt like the American diet. Garlic is having nutrients which lower bad cholesterol, promote healthy immune functioning, lowers risk of cancer. Herbs are also antioxidants in nature and can avoid various diseases.

8. Limit Meat Consumption

The regular Mediterranean diet doesn't have a high content of meats apart from religious events. Even when meat is used, it is grass-fed and pasture-raised and contains a higher amount of Omega-3 fatty acids and CLA.

9. Eat Pasta

Pasta is made from durum and is less likely to spike-up your blood sugar levels. You can combine pasta and olive oil for slowing down absorption.

10. Socialize you're Eating habits

There is no concept of fast food in the Mediterranean diet, so you don't have to eat alone, rather prefer eating with your family and loved ones to have a better taste of food and life.

Chapter 3: Foods to Eat

The Mediterranean diet has vast delicious food options for its followers. The exact foods for the diet seem to be controversial as there is certainly variation between the counties. The foods which are preferred to be consumed for perfectly following the Mediterranean diet include:

- Veggies like, kale, carrots, broccoli, tomatoes, cauliflower, Brussels sprouts, spinach, cucumbers, etc.
- Fruits like oranges, strawberries, figs, peaches, melons, pears, apples, dates, bananas, grapes, etc.
- Seeds and nuts like macadamia nuts, cashews, pumpkin seeds, almonds, walnuts, hazelnuts, sunflower seeds etc.
- Legumes like lentils, chickpeas, beans, pulses, peas, peanuts, etc.
- Tubers like yams, sweet potatoes, turnips, potatoes etc.
- Poultry like turkey, chicken, duck, etc.
- Dairy products like Greek yogurt, cheese, yogurt, etc.
- Eggs like quail eggs, duck eggs, and chicken eggs, etc.
- Spices and Herbs like basil, rosemary, nutmeg, pepper, mint, garlic, sage, cinnamon, etc.
- Healthy fats like avocado oil, olive oil, olives, and avocados, etc.
- Whole grains like rye, corn, barley, wheat oats, whole wheat, pasta and braid (whole grain), corn, brown rice, etc.
- Seafood and Fish like tuna, trout, shrimp, clams, trout, crabs, sardines, mussels, salmon, etc.
- Beverages: The preferred beverage for the Mediterranean diet is water. Apart from this, you can have approximately 1-2 glasses of wine too daily. But you should wine if you have any complications related to its intake. You can also drink tea and coffee, but it's preferable to avoid high-sugar drinks, sugar-sweetened beverages, and various fruit juices.

The important factors regarding food that should be kept in mind while following the Mediterranean diet are:

- ➢ Rarely eat red meat.
- ➢ Moderately eat dairy products and poultry.

➤ You can eat the rest of the foods in abundance.

Chapter 4: Foods to Avoid:

As stated earlier, the Mediterranean diet has vast delicious food options for its followers but there is are certain limitations to it too. The foods which are preferred to be avoided for perfectly following the Mediterranean diet include:

- Added sugars like soda, ice cream, soda, table sugar, and various other same products, etc.
- Refined grains like past (having refined wheat), white bread, etc.
- Trans Fats containing foods like margarine and other processed foods.
- Refined oils like cottonseed oil, canola oil, soybean oil, etc.
- Processed meats like hot dogs, processed sausages, etc.
- Highly processed foods i.e. anything labeled "low-fat" or "diet", which indicates that they have been manufactured in a factory.

Chapter 5: Breakfast Recipes

Avocado Toast

Preparation Time: 15 minutes
Cooking Time: 4 minutes
Servings: 4
Ingredients:
- 1 large avocado, peeled, pitted and chopped roughly
- ¼ teaspoon fresh lemon juice
- 2 tablespoons fresh mint leaves, chopped finely
- Salt and ground black pepper, as required
- 4 large rye bread slices
- 4 hard-boiled eggs, peeled and sliced
- 2 tablespoons feta cheese, crumbled

Method:
1. In a bowl, add the avocado and with a fork, mash roughly.
2. Add lemon juice, mint, salt and black pepper and stir to combine well and keep aside.
3. Heat a nonstick frying pan on medium-high heat and toast the slice for about 2 minutes per side.
4. Repeat with the remaining slices.
5. Spread the avocado mixture over each slice evenly.
6. Sprinkle with feta and serve immediately.

Nutritional Value:
- Calories 197
- Total Fat 15.4 g
- Saturated Fat 4.2 g
- Cholesterol 168 mg
- Total Carbs 8.5 g
- Sugar 1.1 g
- Fiber 4 g
- Sodium 203 mg
- Potassium 331 mg
- Protein 7.9 g

Figs with Yogurt

Preparation Time: 15 minutes
Cooking Time: 7 minutes
Servings: 4
Ingredients:

- 3 tablespoons honey, divided
- 8 ounces fresh figs, halved
- 2 cups plain Greek yogurt
- ¼ cup pistachios, chopped
- Pinch of ground cinnamon

Method:

1. In a medium skillet, add 1 tablespoon of the honey over medium heat and cook for about 1-2 minutes or until heated.
2. Add the figs, cut sides down and cook for about 5 minutes or until caramelized.
3. Remove from the heat and set aside for about 2-3 minutes.
4. Divide the yogurt into serving bowls and top with the caramelized figs.
5. Sprinkle with the pistachios and cinnamon.
6. Drizzle with the remaining honey and serve.

Nutritional Value:

- Calories 319
- Total Fat 9.3 g
- Saturated Fat 4.8 g
- Cholesterol 25 mg
- Total Carbs 57.8 g
- Sugar 47.9 g
- Fiber 6 g
- Sodium 101 mg
- Potassium 663 mg
- Protein 7.2 g

Dried Fruit Couscous

Preparation Time: 10 minutes

Cooking Time: 3 minutes

Servings: 4

Ingredients:

- 3 cups milk
- 1 cup uncooked whole-wheat couscous
- ¼ cup dried currants
- 1/3 cup dried apricots, chopped
- 6 teaspoons dark brown sugar, divided
- ¼ teaspoon ground cinnamon
- Salt, as required
- 2 teaspoons unsalted butter, melted

Method:

1. In a pan, add the milk over medium-high heat and heat for about 2-3 minutes.
2. Remove from the heat and immediately, stir in the couscous, dried fruit, 4 teaspoons of the brown sugar, cinnamon and salt.
3. Set aside, covered for about 15 minutes.
4. In 4 serving bowls, divide the couscous mixture and top with melted butter and remaining brown sugar evenly.
5. Serve immediately.

Nutritional Value:

- Calories 299
- Total Fat 6 g
- Saturated Fat 3.5 g
- Cholesterol 20 mg
- Total Carbs 49.4 g
- Sugar 14.3 g
- Fiber 2.8 g
- Sodium 144 mg
- Potassium 237 mg
- Protein 11.8 g

Veggie Omelet

Preparation Time: 15 minutes
Cooking Time: 15 minutes
Servings: 4
Ingredients:

- 1 teaspoon olive oil
- 2 cups fresh fennel bulbs, sliced thinly
- ¼ cup canned artichoke hearts, rinsed, drained and chopped
- ¼ cup green olives, pitted and chopped
- 1 Roma tomato, chopped
- 6 eggs
- Salt and ground black pepper, as required
- ½ cup goat cheese, crumbled

Method:

1. Preheat the oven to 325 degrees F.
2. In a large ovenproof skillet, heat the oil over medium-high heat and sauté the fennel bulb for about 5 minutes.
3. Stir in the artichoke, olives and tomato and cook for about 3 minutes.
4. Meanwhile, in a bowl, add the eggs, salt and black pepper and beat till well combined.
5. Place the egg mixture over veggie mixture and stir to combine.
6. Cook for about 2 minutes.
7. Sprinkle with the goat cheese evenly and immediately, transfer the skillet into the oven.
8. Bake for about 5 minutes or until eggs are set completely.
9. Remove the skillet from oven and transfer the omelet onto a platter.
10. Cut into desired sized wedges and serve.

Nutritional Value:

- Calories 266
- Total Fat 18.8 g
- Saturated Fat 9.2 g
- Cholesterol 275 mg
- Total Carbs 7.5 g
- Sugar 2.4 g

- Fiber 2.3 g
- Sodium 332 mg
- Potassium 386 mg
- Protein 18.1 g

Veggies & Chickpeas Hash

Preparation Time: 20 minutes
Cooking Time: 15 minutes
Servings: 4
Ingredients:

- 2 tablespoons extra-virgin olive oil
- 2 russet potatoes, chopped
- 1 small onion, chopped
- 2 garlic cloves, chopped
- Salt and ground black pepper, as required
- 1-pound baby asparagus, trimmed and cut into ¼-inch pieces
- 1 cup canned chickpeas, drained and rinsed
- 1 teaspoon dried oregano, crushed
- 1 teaspoon Za'atar
- 1 teaspoon ground allspice
- 1 teaspoon ground coriander
- 1 teaspoon paprika
- Pinch of sugar
- 1 teaspoon white vinegar
- 4 eggs
- 2 Roma tomatoes, chopped
- 1 small red onion, chopped finely
- ½ cup fresh parsley, chopped
- ½ cup feta cheese, crumbled

Method:

1. In a large cast-iron skillet, heat the oil over medium-high heat and cook the potatoes, yellow onion, garlic, salt and black pepper for about 5-7 minutes, stirring frequently.
2. Stir in the asparagus, chickpeas, thyme, spices, sugar and a pinch of salt and black pepper and cook for about 6-8 minutes.
3. Meanwhile, in a medium pan of the water, add the vinegar and bring to a simmer.
4. Crack the eggs, one at a time into a bowl and carefully slide into the pan of water.
5. Cook for about 3 minutes.

6. Carefully, remove the eggs from the water and place onto kitchen towel-lined plate to drain.
7. Sprinkle the eggs with salt and black pepper.
8. Remove the potato hash from the heat and gently, stir in the tomatoes, red onion, parsley and feta.
9. Divide the hash mixture onto serving plates evenly.
10. Top with the poached eggs and serve.

Nutritional Value:

- Calories 485
- Total Fat 19 g
- Saturated Fat 5.6 g
- Cholesterol 180 mg
- Total Carbs 60.2 g
- Sugar 13.2 g
- Fiber 15.9 g
- Sodium 340 mg
- Potassium 1440 mg
- Protein 23.5 g

Eggs with Veggies

Preparation Time: 15 minutes
Cooking Time: 1 hour 20 minutes
Servings: 6
Ingredients:

- 2 tablespoons butter
- 4 small yellow onions, sliced
- 1/3 cup sun-dried tomatoes, julienned
- 1 garlic clove, minced
- 6 large eggs
- 3 ounces feta cheese, crumbled
- Salt and ground black pepper, as required
- 2 tablespoons fresh parsley, chopped

Method:

1. In a large cast iron skillet, melt the butter over medium heat and stir in the onions, spreading in an even layer.
2. Reduce the heat to low and cook for about one hour, stirring after every 5-10 minutes.
3. Add the sun-dried tomatoes and garlic and cook for about 2-3 minutes, stirring frequently.
4. With the spoon, spread the mixture in an even layer.
5. Carefully, crack the eggs over onion mixture and sprinkle with the feta cheese, salt, and black pepper.
6. Cover the pan tightly and cook for about 10-15 minutes or until desired doneness of the eggs.
7. Serve hot with the garnishing of the parsley.

Nutritional Value:

- Calories 165
- Total Fat 11.9 g
- Saturated Fat 6.1 g
- Cholesterol 209 mg
- Total Carbs 6 g
- Sugar 3.2 g
- Fiber 1.2 g
- Sodium 286 mg
- Potassium 178 mg
- Protein 9 g

Quinoa & Veggie Muffins

Preparation Time: 20 minutes
Cooking Time: 35 minutes
Servings: 12
Ingredients:

- 2 teaspoons sunflower oil
- ½ cup onion, chopped finely
- 1 cup cherry tomatoes, sliced
- 2 cups fresh baby spinach, chopped finely
- ½ cup kalamata olives, pitted and chopped
- 1 tablespoon fresh oregano, chopped
- 8 eggs
- 1 cup cooked quinoa
- 1 cup feta cheese, crumbled
- Salt, as required

Method:

1. Preheat the oven to 350 degrees F. Grease a 12 cups muffin tin.
2. In a skillet, heat the oil over medium heat and sauté onion for about 2-3 minutes.
3. Add the tomatoes and sauté for about 1 minute.
4. Add the spinach and sauté for about 1 minute.
5. Remove from the heat and stir in the olives and oregano.
6. In a bowl, crack the eggs and beat slightly.
7. Add the quinoa, feta cheese, veggie mixture and salt and mix until well combined.
8. Divide the mixture into prepared muffin cups evenly.
9. Bake for about 30 minutes or until tops become light golden brown.
10. Remove from the oven and set aside to cool for about 5 minutes before serving.

Nutritional Value:

- Calories 147
- Total Fat 7.9 g
- Saturated Fat 3.1 g
- Cholesterol 120 mg
- Total Carbs 11.6 g
- Sugar 1.4 g
- Fiber 1.7 g
- Sodium 247 mg
- Potassium 204 mg
- Protein 7.9 g

Oats & Yogurt Pancakes

Preparation Time: 15 minutes
Cooking Time: 24 minutes
Servings: 6
Ingredients:

- ½ cup all-purpose flour
- 1 cup old-fashioned oats
- 2 tablespoons flax seeds
- 1 teaspoon baking soda
- Salt, as required
- 2 tablespoons agave syrup
- 2 large eggs
- 2 cups plain Greek yogurt
- 2 tablespoons canola oil

Method:

1. In a blender, add flour, oats, flax seeds, baking soda and salt and pulse until well combined.
2. Transfer the mixture into a large bowl.
3. Add the remaining ingredients except the oil and mix until well combined.
4. Set aside for about 20 minutes before cooking.
5. Heat a large nonstick skillet over medium heat and grease with a little oil.
6. Add ¼ cup of the mixture and cook for about 2 minutes or until bottom becomes golden brown.
7. Carefully, flip the side and cook for about 2 minutes more.
8. Repeat with the remaining mixture.

Nutritional Value:

- Calories 245
- Total Fat 9 g
- Saturated Fat 2 g
- Cholesterol 67 mg
- Total Carbs 29.1 g
- Sugar 6.1 g
- Fiber 2.2 g
- Sodium 325 mg
- Potassium 296 mg
- Protein 10 g

Chapter 6: Soup, Salads & Sandwich Recipes

Tomato Soup

Preparation Time: 15 minutes
Cooking Time: 18 minutes
Servings: 8
Ingredients:

- 3 tablespoons olive oil
- 2 medium yellow onions, sliced thinly
- Salt, as required
- 3 teaspoons curry powder
- 1 teaspoon ground cumin
- 1 teaspoon ground coriander
- ½ teaspoon red pepper flakes
- 1 (15-ounce) can diced tomatoes with juices
- 1 (28-ounce) can plum tomatoes with juices
- 5½ cups vegetable broth
- ½ cup ricotta cheese, crumbled

Method:

1. In a Dutch oven, heat the oil over medium-low heat and cook the onion with 1 teaspoon of the salt for about 10-12 minutes, stirring occasionally.
2. Stir in the curry powder, cumin, coriander and red pepper flakes and cook sauté for about 1 minute.
3. Stir in the tomatoes with juices and broth and simmer for about 15 minutes.
4. Remove from the heat and with a hand blender, blend the soup until smooth.
5. Serve immediately with the topping of ricotta cheese.

Nutritional Value:

- Calories 140
- Total Fat 7.9 g
- Saturated Fat 1.8 g
- Cholesterol 5 mg
- Total Carbs 11.8 g
- Sugar 7.1 g
- Fiber 2.6 g
- Sodium 581 mg
- Potassium 548 mg
- Protein 7.2 g

Beans & Spinach Soup

Preparation Time: 15 minutes
Cooking Time: 25 minutes
Servings: 4
Ingredients:

- 1 tablespoon olive oil
- 1 celery stalk, chopped
- 1 onion, chopped
- 1 garlic clove, minced
- ¼ teaspoon dried thyme, crushed
- 2 (16-ounce) cans white kidney beans, drained and rinsed
- 2 cups vegetable broth
- 2 cups water
- 3 cups fresh spinach, chopped
- Salt and ground black pepper, as required
- 1 tablespoon fresh lemon juice

Method:

1. In a large soup pan, heat oil over medium heat and sauté celery and onion for about 4-5 minutes.
2. Add the garlic and thyme sauté for about 1 minute.
3. Stir in the beans, broth and water and bring to a boil.
4. Reduce the heat to low and simmer for about 15 minutes.
5. Remove from the heat and with a slotted spoon, transfer about 2 cups of the bean's mixture into a bowl.
6. Set aside to cool slightly.
7. In a blender add the slightly cooled beans mixture and pulse until smooth.
8. Return the pureed mixture in the soup and stir to combine.
9. Place the pan over medium heat and stir in the spinach, salt and black pepper.
10. Cook for about 3-4 minutes.
11. Stir in the lemon juice and serve hot.

Nutritional Value:

- Calories 278
- Total Fat 4.3 g
- Saturated Fat 0.7 g
- Cholesterol 0 mg

- Total Carbs 41 g
- Sugar 3.5 g
- Fiber 18.7 g

- Sodium 540 mg
- Potassium 813 mg
- Protein 17.4 g

Lamb, Lentils & Chickpeas Soup

Preparation Time: 15 minutes
Cooking Time: 2¼ hours
Servings: 6
Ingredients:

- 1½ pounds boneless lamb shoulder, cubed
- Salt and ground black pepper, as required
- 2 tablespoons olive oil
- 1 onion, chopped
- 2 garlic cloves, chopped
- 2 tablespoons tomato paste
- 2 teaspoons sweet paprika
- 1½ teaspoons ground cumin
- ½ teaspoon ground cloves
- 2 (14-ounce) cans diced tomatoes
- ¼ cup fresh cilantro, chopped and divided
- 4 cups chicken broth
- 2 (14-ounce) cans brown lentils, rinsed and drained
- 2 (14-ounce) cans chickpeas, rinsed and drained
- 1/3 cup plain Greek yogurt

Method:

1. Season the lamb cubes with salt and black pepper evenly.
2. In a large pan, heat the oil over medium-high heat and sear the lamb cubes in 2 batches for about 4-5 minutes.
3. With a slotted spoon, transfer the lamb cubes into a bowl.
4. In the same pan, add the onion and garlic over medium heat and sauté for about 3-4 minutes.
5. Add the cooked lamb, tomato paste and spices and cook for about 1 minute.
6. Stir in the tomatoes, cilantro and broth and bring to a boil.
7. Reduce the heat to low and simmer, covered for about 1 hour.
8. Stir in the lentils and chickpeas and simmer, covered for about 30 minutes.
9. Uncover and simmer for about 30 minutes more.
10. Stir in the salt and black pepper and remove from the heat.

11. Serve hot with the topping of yogurt.

Nutritional Value:

- Calories 562
- Total Fat 15.3 g
- Saturated Fat 4.3 g
- Cholesterol 103 mg
- Total Carbs 49.2 g
- Sugar 8.2 g
- Fiber 14.8 g
- Sodium 911 mg
- Potassium 979 mg
- Protein 53.6 g

Chicken & Orzo Soup

Preparation Time: 10 minutes
Cooking Time: 20 minutes
Servings: 8
Ingredients:

- 1 tablespoon olive oil
- 1½ pounds skinless, boneless chicken breasts, cubed into ¾-inch size
- 1 tablespoon Greek seasoning
- Ground black pepper, as required
- 4 scallions, sliced thinly
- 1 garlic clove, minced
- ¼ cup white wine
- ¼ cup Greek olives, pitted and sliced
- ¼ cup sun-dried tomatoes, chopped
- 1 tablespoon capers, drained
- 1½ teaspoons fresh oregano, minced
- 1½ teaspoons fresh basil, minced
- 7 cups chicken broth
- 1½ cups uncooked orzo pasta
- 2 tablespoons fresh lemon juice
- 2 teaspoons fresh parsley, chopped finely

Method:

1. In a Dutch oven, heat the oil over medium heat and cook the chicken breasts with Greek seasoning and black pepper for about 4-5 minutes or until golden brown from both sides.
2. With a slotted spoon, transfer the chicken breasts onto a plate and set aside.
3. In the same pan, add the scallions and garlic and sauté for about 1 minute.
4. Add the wine and remove the brown bits from the bottom of pan.
5. Stir in the cooked chicken, olives, tomatoes, capers, oregano, basil and broth and bring to a boil.
6. Reduce the heat to low and simmer, covered for about 15 minutes.
7. Increase the heat to medium and again bring to a boil.
8. Stir in orzo and cook for about 8-10 minutes or until desired doneness of the pasta.

9. Stir in the lemon juice and parsley and serve hot.

Nutritional Value:

- Calories 298
- Total Fat 10.1 g
- Saturated Fat 2.5 g
- Cholesterol 76 mg
- Total Carbs 17.4 g
- Sugar 1.5 g
- Fiber 0.6 g
- Sodium 875 mg
- Potassium 450 mg
- Protein 31.4 g

Fresh Veggie Salad

Preparation Time: 15 minutes

Servings: 6

Ingredients:

- 2 cucumbers, peeled and chopped
- 3 large ripe tomatoes, chopped
- ½ cup black olives, pitted and sliced
- 1 small red onion, chopped
- 4 teaspoons fresh lemon juice
- ¼ cup extra-virgin olive oil
- 1½ teaspoon dried oregano, crushed
- Salt and ground black pepper, as required
- 1 cup feta cheese, crumbled

Method:

1. In a large serving bowl, add all the ingredients except feta and toss to coat well.
2. Top with the feta and serve immediately.

Nutritional Value:

- Calories 189
- Total Fat 15.3 g
- Saturated Fat 5.2 g
- Cholesterol 22 mg
- Total Carbs 10.3 g
- Sugar 5.7 g
- Fiber 2.4 g
- Sodium 411 mg
- Potassium 407 mg
- Protein 5.3 g

Chickpeas Salad

Preparation Time: 15 minutes
Servings: 6
Ingredients:
For Salad:

- 2 (15-ounce) cans chickpeas, rinsed and drained
- 2½ cups cherry tomatoes, halved
- ½ green bell pepper, cored and chopped
- ½ cup sun-dried tomatoes, chopped
- ¼ cup green olives, pitted
- ¼ cup Kalamata olives, pitted
- 4 scallions, chopped
- ½ cup fresh mint leaves, chopped
- ½ cup fresh parsley leaves, chopped

For Dressing:

- ¼ cup extra-virgin olive oil
- 2 tablespoons fresh lemon juice
- 2 tablespoons white wine vinegar
- 1 garlic clove, minced
- 1 teaspoon ground sumac
- ½ teaspoon red pepper flakes, crushed
- Salt and ground black pepper, as required

Method:

1. For salad: in a large serving bowl, add all the ingredients and mix.
2. For dressing: in another bowl, add all the ingredients and beat until well combined.
3. Place the dressing over the salad and gently, toss to coat.
4. Set aside for about 30 minutes.
5. Gently, stir the salad and serve.

Nutritional Value:

- Calories 242
- Total Fat 11.8 g
- Saturated Fat 1.5 g
- Cholesterol 0 mg
- Total Carbs 28.8 g
- Sugar 6.9 g
- Fiber 7.6 g
- Sodium 558 mg

- Potassium 45 mg

- Protein 8 g

Tuna Salad

Preparation Time: 20 minutes
Servings: 6
Ingredients:
For Vinaigrette:

- 3 tablespoons fresh lime juice
- 1/3 cup extra-virgin olive oil
- 2½ teaspoons Dijon mustard
- 1 teaspoon fresh lime zest, grated
- ½ teaspoon ground sumac
- ½ teaspoon red pepper flakes, crushed
- Salt and ground black pepper, as required

For Salad:

- 3 (5-ounce) cans tuna in olive oil
- 2½ celery stalks, chopped
- 4 whole small radishes, stemmed and chopped
- ½ of cucumber, chopped
- ½ cup Kalamata olives, pitted and halved
- ½ of medium red onion, chopped finely
- 3 scallions, chopped
- 1 cup fresh parsley, chopped finely
- ½ cup fresh mint leaves, chopped

Method:

1. For vinaigrette: in a bowl, add all the ingredients and beat until well combined.
2. For salad: in a large serving bowl, add all the ingredients and mix.
3. Place the dressing over the salad and gently, toss to coat.
4. Refrigerate, covered for about 30-40 minutes before serving.

Nutritional Value:

- Calories 266
- Total Fat 18.7 g
- Saturated Fat 3 g
- Cholesterol 22 mg

- Total Carbs 5.2 g
- Sugar 1.3 g
- Fiber 2.2 g

- Sodium 276 mg
- Potassium 435 mg
- Protein 20.3 g

Grilled Veggie Sandwiches

Preparation Time: 25 minutes
Cooking Time: 5 minutes
Servings: 4
Ingredients:

- ¼ cup mayonnaise
- ½ teaspoon fresh lemon juice
- 2 garlic cloves, minced
- 2 small zucchinis, sliced thinly lengthwise
- 1 eggplant, cut into ¼-inch thick slices
- 2 portabella mushrooms, cut into ¼-inch thick slices
- 2 tablespoons olive oil
- Salt, as required
- ¾ of a ciabatta loaf, split horizontally
- ½ cup feta cheese, crumbled
- 2 medium tomatoes, sliced
- 2 cups fresh baby arugula

Method:

1. Preheat the grill to high heat. Grease the grill grate.
2. In a bowl, add the mayonnaise, lemon juice and garlic and mix well.
3. Set aside until using.
4. Coat the zucchini, eggplant and mushrooms with oil evenly and then, sprinkle with salt.
5. Grill the vegetable slices for about 1½ minutes per side.
6. Transfer the vegetable slices onto a plate.
7. Now, place the bread onto grill, cut side down and grill for about 2 minutes.
8. Cut each loaf half into 4 equal sized pieces.
9. Spread the mayonnaise mixture over bottom of each piece and top with the vegetable slices, followed by the tomatoes, arugula and cheese.
10. Cover with top pieces and serve.

Nutritional Value:

- Calories 361
- Total Fat 18.1 g
- Saturated Fat 4.9 g
- Cholesterol 21 mg

- Total Carbs 43 g
- Sugar 10.9 g
- Fiber 7.4 g

- Sodium 701 mg
- Potassium 862 mg
- Protein 10.3 g

Chicken Sandwiches

Preparation Time: 25 minutes
Cooking Time: 15 minutes
Servings: 4
Ingredients:
For Aioli:

- 1 (6½-ounce) jar marinated artichoke hearts, drained
- 2 tablespoons Parmesan cheese, grated
- 2 tablespoons mayonnaise
- 1 tablespoon fresh lemon juice
- ½ teaspoon fresh lemon zest, grated
- ¼ teaspoon red pepper flakes, crushed
- Salt and ground black pepper, as required

For Sandwiches:

- 4 (4-ounce) skinless, boneless chicken breast halves, cubed
- 1 tablespoon garlic, minced
- 1 tablespoon olive oil
- 1 teaspoon red pepper flakes, crushed
- Pinch of salt and ground black pepper
- 1 onion, chopped
- 1 yellow bell pepper, seeded and chopped
- ¼ cup capers, drained
- ¼ cup kalamata olives, pitted and chopped
- 1 cup cherry tomatoes, halved
- ½ pound mozzarella cheese, shredded
- 1 cup feta cheese, crumbled
- 4 hoagie buns, split lengthwise and toasted
- ¼ cup fresh basil, chopped

Method:

1. For aioli: in a food processor, add all the ingredients and pulse until smooth.
2. Transfer the aioli into a bowl and refrigerate, covered before serving.
3. For sandwiches: in a large bowl, add the chicken, garlic, oil, red pepper flakes, salt and black pepper and toss to coat well.

4. Heat a large pan over medium-high heat and cook the chicken mixture for about 5 minutes, stirring frequently.
5. Add the onion and bell pepper and cook for about 5 minutes.
6. Add the capers and olives and stir to combine.
7. Add the mozzarella cheese and stir until melted completely.
8. Remove from the heat and stir in the feta cheese.
9. Spread the aioli over each hoagie roll evenly.
10. Place the chicken mixture over bottom half of each bun and top with the basil.
11. Cover with top half of each bun and serve.

Nutritional Value:

- Calories 548
- Total Fat 22.9 g
- Saturated Fat 9 g
- Cholesterol 105 mg
- Total Carbs 47.5 g
- Sugar 10.9 g
- Fiber 6.3 g
- Sodium 1200 mg
- Potassium 433 mg
- Protein 40.1 g

Lamb Sandwiches

Preparation Time: 15 minutes
Cooking Time: 6 minutes
Servings: 4
Ingredients:

- ¾ pound boneless leg of lamb, cut into bite sized pieces
- 2 teaspoons olive oil
- 2 garlic cloves, minced
- 1 tablespoon fresh rosemary, minced
- Salt and ground black pepper, as required
- 1 (6-ounce) container plain Greek yogurt
- 1½ cups cucumber, chopped finely
- 1 tablespoon fresh lemon juice
- 4 (6-inch) whole-wheat pita breads, warmed

Method:

1. In a bowl, add the lamb pieces, garlic, rosemary, salt and black pepper and toss to coat well.
2. In a large nonstick skillet, heat oil over medium-high heat and stir fry the lamb mixture for about 5-6 minutes or until desired doneness.
3. Remove from the heat and set aside.
4. For yogurt sauce: in a bowl, add the yogurt, cucumber, lemon juice, salt and black pepper and mix well.
5. Divide the lamb mixture between pitas evenly and serve immediately with the drizzling of the yogurt sauce.

Nutritional Value:

- Calories 390
- Total Fat 11 g
- Saturated Fat 3.4 g
- Cholesterol 79 mg
- Total Carbs 40.7 g
- Sugar 4.3 g
- Fiber 5.3 g
- Sodium 476 mg
- Potassium 569 mg
- Protein 33 g

Chapter 7: Snack Recipes

Date Smoothie

Preparation Time: 10 minutes

Servings: 2

Ingredients:

- 6 Medjool dates, pitted and chopped roughly
- 1 cup plain Greek yogurt
- 2 tablespoons almond butter
- 1 cup fresh apple juice
- ½ cup ice cubes

Method:

1. In a high-speed blender, add all ingredients and pulse until smooth and creamy.
2. Place the smoothie into 2 serving glasses and serve.

Nutritional Value:

- Calories 482
- Total Fat 10.7 g
- Saturated Fat 2 g
- Cholesterol 7 mg
- Total Carbs 88.6 g
- Sugar 75.3 g
- Fiber 7.9 g
- Sodium 92 mg
- Potassium 532 mg
- Protein 13.5 g

Stuffed Tomatoes

Preparation Time: 15 minutes
Cooking Time: 5 minutes
Servings: 4
Ingredients:

- 2 large tomatoes, halved crosswise
- ¼ cup kalamata olives, pitted and sliced
- 2 tablespoons fresh basil, chopped
- ¼ cup goat cheese, crumbled
- ½ cup garlic croutons
- 2 tablespoons balsamic vinaigrette

Method:

1. Preheat the broiler of the oven. Arrange the oven rack about 4-5-nch from the heating element.
2. With your fingers, remove the seeds from the tomato halves.
3. Carefully, run a small knife around the pulp vertically, not touching the bottom and then, gently remove the pulp.
4. Chop the tomato pulp and transfer into a bowl.
5. Arrange the tomatoes over the paper towels, cut side down to drain.
6. In the bowl of tomato pulp, add the remaining ingredients and mix well.
7. Stuff the tomatoes with olive mixture evenly.
8. Arrange the tomatoes onto a broiler pan and broil for about 5 minutes or until cheese is melted
9. Serve warm.

Nutritional Value:

- Calories 199
- Total Fat 14.4 g
- Saturated Fat 7.7 g
- Cholesterol 30 mg
- Total Carbs 8 g
- Sugar 3.5 g
- Fiber 1.6 g
- Sodium 262 mg
- Potassium 238 mg
- Protein 10 g

Tomato Bruschetta

Preparation Time: 20 minutes
Cooking Time: 1 minute 40 seconds
Servings: 8
Ingredients:

- 2 cups fresh tomatoes, chopped
- 2 tablespoons fresh basil, chopped
- 4 garlic cloves, minced
- Salt, as required
- 1 crusty bread loaf, cut into 16 (¾-inch thick) pieces
- 2 tablespoons olive oil
- 1-ounce mozzarella cheese, shredded

Method:

1. In a bowl, add the tomatoes, basil, garlic, and salt and gently, toss them to coat.
2. Set aside for about 5-10 minutes.
3. Preheat the broiler of the oven. Grease a large baking sheet.
4. Arrange the bread slices onto the prepared baking sheet in a single layer.
5. Coat the top of each bread slice with a little oil and broil for about 1 minute.
6. Remove from the oven and top each slice with about 2 tablespoons of the tomato mixture, followed by the mozzarella cheese.
7. Broil for about 30-40 seconds more.
8. Remove from the oven and transfer tonto a platter.
9. Set aside to cool for a few minutes before serving.

Nutritional Value:

- Calories 140
- Total Fat 5.4 g
- Saturated Fat 0.9 g
- Cholesterol 2 mg
- Total Carbs 20.4 g
- Sugar 2.7 g
- Fiber 1.1 g
- Sodium 268 mg
- Potassium 115 mg
- Protein 4.5 g

Zucchini & Quinoa Fritters

Preparation Time: 25 minutes
Cooking Time: 26 minutes
Servings: 14
Ingredients:

- 1 cup water
- ½ cup quinoa
- 2 cups zucchini, grated
- Salt, as required
- 1 cup panko breadcrumbs
- 1 cup Parmigiano-Reggiano cheese, grated
- 1 egg
- 3 garlic cloves, minced
- ½ teaspoon dried oregano
- Ground black pepper, as required
- 3 tablespoons olive oil

Method:

1. In a small pan, add the water and quinoa over medium-high heat and bring to a boil.
2. Reduce the heat to low and simmer, covered for about 10 minutes.
3. Remove from the heat and with fork, fluff the quinoa.
4. Set aside for about 10 minutes.
5. Meanwhile, in a colander, place the zucchini and ½ teaspoon of salt and toss to coat.
6. Arrange the colander over a sink for at least 10 minutes.
7. With paper towels, pat dry the zucchini.
8. In a large bowl, add the zucchini, quinoa, breadcrumbs, cheese, egg, garlic, oregano, salt and black pepper and mix until well combined.
9. Make 2½-inch patties from the mixture and with your hands, flatten each slightly.
10. In a large skillet, heat the oil over medium heat and cook the patties in 2 batches for about 4 minutes per side or until golden brown.
11. Transfer the fritters onto a paper towel-lined plate to drain.
12. Serve warm.

Nutritional Value:

- Calories 110
- Total Fat 15.8 g
- Saturated Fat 1.8 g
- Cholesterol 16 mg
- Total Carbs 10.3 g
- Sugar 0.8 g
- Fiber 1 g
- Sodium 109 mg
- Potassium 99 mg
- Protein 4.8 g

Chickpeas Falafel

Preparation Time: 15 minutes
Cooking Time: 6 minutes
Servings: 8
Ingredients:

- 1 (15½-ounce) can chickpeas, rinsed and drained
- 1 garlic clove, chopped
- ½ cup fresh parsley, chopped roughly
- ¼ teaspoon ground cumin
- Salt and ground black pepper, as required
- ¼ cup all-purpose flour, divided
- 1 egg, beaten
- 2 tablespoons olive oil

Method:

1. In a food processor, add the chickpeas, garlic, parsley, cumin, salt and black pepper and pulse until chopped.
2. Transfer the mixture into a bowl.
3. Add 2 tablespoons of flour and egg and mix until well combined.
4. Make 8 equal sized patties from the mixture.
5. In a shallow dish, place remaining flour.
6. Coat the patties with the flour evenly and then, shake off the excess.
7. In a large nonstick skillet, heat oil over medium-high heat and cook the patties for about 2-3 minutes per side or until golden brown.
8. Serve warm.

Nutritional Value:

- Calories 100
- Total Fat 4.8 g
- Saturated Fat 0.7 g
- Cholesterol 20 mg
- Total Carbs 11.1 g
- Sugar 1 g
- Fiber 2.1 g
- Sodium 156 mg
- Potassium 35 mg
- Protein 3.5 g

Beef & Bulgur Meatballs

Preparation Time: 20 minutes
Cooking Time: 28 minutes
Servings: 6
Ingredients:

- ¾ cup uncooked bulgur
- 1-pound ground beef
- ¼ cup shallots, minced
- ¼ cup fresh parsley, minced
- ½ teaspoon ground allspice
- ½ teaspoon ground cumin
- ½ teaspoon ground cinnamon
- ¼ teaspoon red pepper flakes, crushed
- Salt, as required
- 1 tablespoon olive oil

Method:

1. In a large bowl of the cold water, soak the bulgur for about 30 minutes.
2. Drain the bulgur well and then, squeeze with your hands to remove the excess water.
3. In a food processor, add the bulgur, beef, shallot, parsley, spices and salt and pulse until a smooth mixture is formed.
4. Transfer the mixture into a bowl and refrigerate, covered for about 30 minutes.
5. Remove from the refrigerator and make equal sized balls from the beef mixture.
6. In a large nonstick skillet, heat the oil over medium-high heat and cook the meatballs in 2 batches for about 13-14 minutes, flipping frequently.
7. Serve warm.

Nutritional Value:

- Calories 228
- Total Fat 7.4 g
- Saturated Fat 2.2 g
- Cholesterol 68 mg
- Total Carbs 15 g
- Sugar 0.1 g
- Fiber 3.5 g
- Sodium 83 mg
- Potassium 420 mg
- Protein 25.4 g

Feta Dip

Preparation Time: 15 minutes

Servings: 6

Ingredients:

- 1½ cups feta cheese, crumbled
- ½ cup whole milk
- ½ cup walnut pieces, toasted
- 2 tablespoons fresh oregano leaves, chopped
- 1 teaspoon hot sauce
- 1 teaspoon fresh lemon juice
- Ground black pepper, as required
- 1 roasted red pepper, chopped
- ½ cup kalamata olive, pitted and chopped

Method:

1. In a food processor, add the feta, milk, walnuts, oregano, hot sauce, lemon juice and black pepper and pulse until smooth and creamy.
2. Transfer the dip into a serving bowl and serve with the garnishing of the red pepper and olives.

Nutritional Value:

- Calories 197
- Total Fat 16.2 g
- Saturated Fat 6.5 g
- Cholesterol 35 mg
- Total Carbs 5.9 g
- Sugar 3.3 g
- Fiber 1.9 g
- Sodium 575 mg
- Potassium 155 mg
- Protein 8.9 g

Chickpeas Hummus

Preparation Time: 15 minutes

Servings: 4

Ingredients:

- 1 (15-ounce) can chickpeas, rinsed and drained
- 3 garlic cloves, minced
- ½ teaspoon fresh lemon zest, grated
- 1/3 cup olive oil
- 3 tablespoons fresh lemon juice
- 3 tablespoons tahini
- 2 tablespoons plain yogurt
- 1 teaspoon ground cumin
- ¼ teaspoon cayenne pepper
- Salt, as required
- 2 tablespoons pine nuts, chopped

Method:

1. In a food processor, add all the ingredients except the pine nuts and pulse until smooth.
2. Transfer the hummus into a serving bowl and refrigerate, covered for about 1-2 hours.
3. Serve with the topping of the pine nuts.

Nutritional Value:

- Calories 627
- Total Fat 31.1 g
- Saturated Fat 4.2 g
- Cholesterol 0 mg
- Total Carbs 69 g
- Sugar 12.4 g
- Fiber 19.8 g
- Sodium 86 mg
- Potassium 1000 mg
- Protein 23.5 g

Chapter 8: Pizza & Pasta Recipes

Veggie Pizza

Preparation Time: 20 minutes
Cooking Time: 12 minutes
Servings: 6
Ingredients:

- 1 (12-inch) prepared pizza crust
- ¼ teaspoon Italian seasoning
- ¼ teaspoon red pepper flakes, crushed
- 1 cup goat cheese, crumbled
- 1 (14-ounce) can quartered artichoke hearts
- 3 plum tomatoes, sliced into ¼-inch thick size
- 6 kalamata olives, pitted and sliced
- ¼ cup fresh basil, chopped

Method:

1. Preheat the oven to 450 degrees F. Grease a baking sheet.
2. Sprinkle the pizza crust with Italian seasoning and red pepper flakes evenly.
3. Place the goat cheese over crust evenly, leaving about ½-inch of the sides.
4. With the back of a spoon, gently press the cheese downwards.
5. Place the artichoke, tomato and olives on top of the cheese.
6. Arrange the pizza crust onto the prepared baking sheet.
7. Bake for about 10-12 minutes or till cheese becomes bubbly.
8. Remove from oven and sprinkle with the basil.
9. Cut into equal sized wedges and serve.

Nutritional Value:

- Calories 381
- Total Fat 16.1 g
- Saturated Fat 9.8 g
- Cholesterol 40 mg
- Total Carbs 42.4 g
- Sugar 8 g
- Fiber 5.4 g
- Sodium 710 mg
- Potassium 393 mg
- Protein 19.4 g

Chicken Pizza

Preparation Time: 1 minute
Cooking Time: 10 minutes
Servings: 4
Ingredients:

- 2 flatbreads
- 1 tablespoon Greek vinaigrette
- ½ cup feta cheese, crumbled
- ¼ cup Parmesan cheese, grated
- ½ cup water-packed artichoke hearts, rinsed, drained and chopped
- ½ cup olives, pitted and sliced
- ½ cup cooked chicken breast strips, chopped
- 1/8 teaspoon dried basil
- 1/8 teaspoon dried oregano
- Pinch of ground black pepper
- 1 cup part-skim mozzarella cheese, shredded

Method:

1. Preheat the oven to 400 degrees F.
2. Arrange the flatbreads onto a large ungreased baking sheet and coat each with vinaigrette.
3. Top with feta, followed by the Parmesan, veggies and chicken.
4. Sprinkle with dried herbs and black pepper.
5. Top with mozzarella cheese evenly.
6. Bake for about 8-10 minutes or until cheese is melted.
7. Remove from the oven and set aside for about 1-2 minutes before slicing.
8. Cut each flat bread into 2 pieces and serve.

Nutritional Value:

- Calories 393
- Total Fat 22 g
- Saturated Fat 9.5 g
- Cholesterol 84 mg
- Total Carbs 20.6 g
- Sugar 1.8 g
- Fiber 3.9 g
- Sodium 1000 mg
- Potassium 248 mg
- Protein 28.9 g

Beef Pizza

Preparation Time: 25 minutes

Cooking Time: 50 minutes

Servings: 10

Ingredients:

For Crust:

- 3 cups all-purpose flour
- 1 tablespoon sugar
- 2¼ teaspoons active dry yeast
- 1 teaspoon salt
- 2 tablespoons olive oil
- 1 cup warm water

For Topping:

- 1-pound ground beef
- 1 medium onion, chopped
- 2 tablespoons tomato paste
- 1 tablespoon ground cumin
- Salt and ground black pepper, as required
- ¼ cup water
- 1 cup fresh spinach, chopped
- 8 ounces artichoke hearts, quartered
- 4 ounces fresh mushrooms, sliced
- 2 tomatoes, chopped
- 4 ounces feta cheese, crumbled

Method:

1. For crust: in the bowl of a stand mixer, fitted with the dough hook, add the flour, sugar, yeast and salt.
2. Add 2 tablespoons of the oil and warm water and knead until a smooth and elastic dough is formed.
3. Make a ball of the dough and set aside for about 15 minutes.
4. Place the dough onto a lightly floured surface and roll into a circle.
5. Place the dough into a lightly, greased round pizza pan and gently, press to fit.
6. Set aside for about 10-15 minutes.

7. Coat the crust with some oil.
8. Preheat the oven to 400 degrees F.
9. For topping: heat a nonstick skillet over medium-high heat and cook the beef for about 4-5 minutes.
10. Add the onion and cook for about 5 minutes, stirring frequently.
11. Add the tomato paste, cumin, salt, black pepper and water and stir to combine.
12. Reduce the heat to medium and cook for about 5-10 minutes.
13. Remove from the heat and set aside.
14. Place the beef mixture over the pizza crust and top with the spinach, followed by the artichokes, mushrooms, tomatoes, and Feta cheese.
15. Bake for about 25-30 minutes or until the cheese is melted.
16. Remove from the oven and set aside for about 3-5 minutes before slicing.
17. Cut into desired sized slices and serve.

Nutritional Value:

- Calories 309
- Total Fat 8.7 g
- Saturated Fat 3.3 g
- Cholesterol 51 mg
- Total Carbs 36.4 g
- Sugar 3.7 g
- Fiber 3.3 g
- Sodium 421 mg
- Potassium 502 mg
- Protein 21.4 g

Shrimp Pizza

Preparation Time: 15 minutes

Cooking Time: 10 minutes

Serving: 1

Ingredients:

- 2 tablespoons spaghetti sauce
- 1 tablespoon pesto sauce
- 1 (6-inch) pita bread
- 2 tablespoons mozzarella cheese, shredded
- 5 cherry tomatoes, halved
- 1/8 cup bay shrimp
- Pinch of garlic powder
- Pinch of dried basil

Method:

1. Preheat the oven to 325 degrees F. Lightly, grease a baking sheet.
2. In a bowl, mix together the spaghetti sauce and pesto.
3. Spread the pesto mixture over the pita bread in a thin layer.
4. Top the pita bread with the cheese, followed by the tomatoes and shrimp.
5. Sprinkle with the garlic powder and basil.
6. Arrange the pita bread onto the prepared baking sheet and bake for about 7-10 minutes.
7. Remove from the oven and set aside for about 3-5 minutes before slicing.
8. Cut into desired sized slices and serve.

Nutritional Value:

- Calories 482
- Total Fat 18.9 g
- Saturated Fat 7.8 g
- Cholesterol 119 mg
- Total Carbs 44.5 g
- Sugar 6.6 g
- Fiber 3.3 g
- Sodium 900 mg
- Potassium 420 mg
- Protein 33.4 g

Herbed Pasta

Preparation Time: 15 minutes
Cooking Time: 15 minutes
Servings: 4
Ingredients:

- 1 (8-ounce) package linguini pasta
- 2 tablespoons olive oil
- 1 tablespoon garlic, minced
- 1 tablespoon dried oregano, crushed
- 1 tablespoon dried basil, crushed
- 1 teaspoon dried thyme, crushed
- 2 cups plum tomatoes, chopped

Method:

1. In a large pan of lightly salted boiling water, add the pasta and cook for about 8-10 minutes or according to package's directions.
2. Drain the pasta well.
3. In a large skillet, heat oil over medium heat and sauté the garlic for about 1 minute.
4. Stir in herbs and sauté for about 1 minute more.
5. Add the pasta and cook for about 2-3 minutes or until heated completely.
6. Fold in tomatoes and remove from heat.
7. Serve hot.

Nutritional Value:

- Calories 301
- Total Fat 8.9 g
- Saturated Fat 1.6 g
- Cholesterol 0 mg
- Total Carbs 47.7 g
- Sugar 4.7 g
- Fiber 6.7 g
- Sodium 12 mg
- Potassium 215 mg
- Protein 8.5 g

Pasta with Veggies

Preparation Time: 15 minutes
Cooking Time: 20 minutes
Servings: 6
Ingredients:

- 3 tomatoes
- 1-pound farfalle pasta
- ¼ cup olive oil
- 1-pound fresh mushrooms, sliced
- 3 garlic cloves, minced
- 1 teaspoon dried oregano, crushed
- 1 (2-ounce) can black olives, drained
- ¾ cup feta cheese, crumbled

Method:

1. In a large pan of the salted boiling water, add the tomatoes and cook for about 1 minute.
2. With a slotted spoon, transfer the tomatoes into a bowl of ice water.
3. In the same pan of the boiling water, add the pasta and cook for about 8-10 minutes.
4. Drain the pasta well.
5. Meanwhile, peel the blanched tomatoes and then chop them.
6. In a large skillet, heat oil over medium heat and sauté the mushrooms and garlic for about 4-5 minutes.
7. Add the tomatoes and oregano and cook for about 3-4 minutes.
8. Divide the pasta onto serving plates and top with mushroom mixture.
9. Garnish with olives and feta and serve.

Nutritional Value:

- Calories 446
- Total Fat 15.1 g
- Saturated Fat 4.2 g
- Cholesterol 17 mg
- Total Carbs 62.2 g
- Sugar 6.4 g
- Fiber 4.6 g
- Sodium 299 mg
- Potassium 409 mg
- Protein 15.2 g

Pasta with Chicken & Veggies

Preparation Time: 15 minutes
Cooking Time: 10 minutes
Servings: 7
Ingredients:

- 3 tablespoons olive oil
- 1-pound boneless, skinless chicken breast, sliced diagonally
- 1 (8½-ounce) jar sun-dried tomatoes, julienned
- 2 tablespoons garlic, minced
- 1-pound angel hair pasta
- 1 (8½-ounce) can water-packed artichoke hearts, quartered and drained
- ½ cup kalamata olive, pitted
- ¼ cup fresh basil
- 6 ounces feta cheese, crumbled
- ¼ cup heavy cream
- 1 teaspoon dried oregano
- Salt and ground black pepper, as required

Method:

1. In a skillet, heat the oil over medium heat and sear the chicken strips for about 5-6 minutes or until browned completely.
2. Add the sun-dried tomatoes and garlic and sauté for about 2 minutes.
3. Meanwhile, in a large pan of the salted boiling water, add the pasta and cook for about 5-6 minutes.
4. Drain the pasta well.
5. In the skillet, add the artichoke hearts, olives, basil and feta cheese and sauté for about 1 minute.
6. Add the cream and stir to combine.
7. Stir in the oregano, salt and black pepper and remove from the heat.
8. In a large serving bowl, add the pasta and chicken mixture and toss to coat well.
9. Serve immediately.

Nutritional Value:

- Calories 429
- Total Fat 17.1 g
- Saturated Fat 5.9 g
- Cholesterol 116 mg

- Total Carbs 43.1 g
- Sugar 2.3 g
- Fiber 2.7 g

- Sodium 464 mg
- Potassium 599 mg
- Protein 26.3 g

Pasta with Shrimp & Spinach

Preparation Time: 15 minutes
Cooking Time: 10 minutes
Servings: 4
Ingredients:

- 1 cup sour cream
- ½ cup feta cheese, crumbled
- 3 garlic cloves, chopped
- 2 teaspoons dried basil, crushed
- ¼ teaspoon red pepper flakes, crushed
- 8 ounces fettuccine pasta
- 1 (10-ounce) packages frozen spinach, thawed
- 12 ounces medium shrimp, peeled and deveined
- Salt and ground black pepper, as required

Method:

1. In a large serving bowl, add the sour cream, feta, garlic, basil, red pepper flakes and salt and mix well.
2. Set aside until using.
3. In a large pan of the lightly salted boiling water, add the fettucine and cook for about 10 minutes or according to the package's directions.
4. After 8 minutes, stir in the spinach and shrimp and cook for about 2 minutes.
5. Drain the pasta mixture well.
6. Add the hot pasta mixture into the bowl of the sour cream mixture and gently, toss to coat.
7. Serve immediately.

Nutritional Value:

- Calories 457
- Total Fat 19.1 g
- Saturated Fat 11 g
- Cholesterol 262 mg
- Total Carbs 38.9 g
- Sugar 1.2 g
- Fiber 1.7 g
- Sodium 557 mg
- Potassium 748 mg
- Protein 32.5 g

Chapter 9: Fish & Seafood Recipes

Salmon with Veggies

Preparation Time: 15 minutes
Cooking Time: 22 minutes
Servings: 4
Ingredients:

- 4 (6-ounce) (1-inch thick) skinless salmon fillets
- Salt and ground black pepper, as required
- 1 (2¼-ounce) can sliced ripe olives, drained
- ½ cup zucchini, chopped finely
- 2 cups cherry tomatoes, halved
- 2 tablespoons canned capers with liquid
- 1 tablespoon olive oil

Method:

1. Preheat the oven to 425 degrees F. Grease an 11x7-inch baking dish
2. Season the salmon fillets with salt and black pepper generously.
3. In a bowl, add the remaining ingredients and toss to coat well.
4. Place the salmon fillets into the prepared baking dish in a single layer and to with the veggie mixture evenly.
5. Bake for about 22 minutes.
6. Serve hot.

Nutritional Value:

- Calories 293
- Total Fat 16 g
- Saturated Fat 2.3 g
- Cholesterol 75 mg
- Total Carbs 5.2 g
- Sugar 2.6 g
- Fiber 1.9 g
- Sodium 386 mg
- Potassium 907 mg
- Protein 34.2 g

Tilapia in Herb Sauce

Preparation Time: 15 minutes
Cooking Time: 14 minutes
Servings: 4
Ingredients:

- 2 (14-ounce) cans diced tomatoes with basil and garlic, undrained
- 1/3 cup fresh parsley, chopped and divided
- ¼ teaspoon dried oregano
- ½ teaspoon red pepper flakes, crushed
- 4 (6-ounce) tilapia fillets
- 2 tablespoons fresh lemon juice
- 2/3 cup feta cheese, crumbled

Method:

1. Preheat the oven to 400 degrees F.
2. In a shallow baking dish, add the tomatoes, ¼ cup of the parsley, oregano and red pepper flakes and mix until well combined.
3. Arrange the tilapia fillets over the tomato mixture in a single layer and drizzle with the lemon juice.
4. Place some tomato mixture over the tilapia fillets and sprinkle with the feta cheese evenly.
5. Bake for about 12-14 minutes.
6. Serve hot with the garnishing of remaining parsley.

Nutritional Value:

- Calories 246
- Total Fat 7.4 g
- Saturated Fat 4.6 g
- Cholesterol 105 mg
- Total Carbs 9.4 g
- Sugar 6.5 g
- Fiber 2.7 g
- Sodium 353 mg
- Potassium 529 mg
- Protein 37.2 g

Tuna with Olives

Preparation Time: 15 minutes

Cooking Time: 14 minutes

Servings: 4

Ingredients:

- 4 (6-ounce) (1-inch thick) tuna steaks
- 2 tablespoons extra-virgin olive oil, divided
- Salt and ground black pepper, as required
- 2 garlic cloves, minced
- 1 cup fresh tomatoes, chopped
- 1 cup dry white wine
- 2/3 cup green olives, pitted and sliced
- ¼ cup capers, drained
- 2 tablespoons fresh thyme, chopped
- 1½ tablespoons fresh lemon zest, grated
- 2 tablespoons fresh lemon juice
- 3 tablespoons fresh parsley, chopped

Method:

1. Preheat the grill to high heat. Grease the grill grate.
2. Coat the tuna steaks with 1 tablespoon of the oil and sprinkle with salt and black pepper.
3. Set aside for about 5 minutes.
4. For sauce: in a small skillet, heat the remaining oil over medium heat and sauté the garlic for about 1 minute.
5. Add the tomatoes and cook for about 2 minutes.
6. Stir in the wine and bring to a boil.
7. Add the remaining ingredients except the parsley and cook, uncovered for about 5 minutes.
8. Stir in the parsley, salt and black pepper and remove from the heat.
9. Meanwhile, grill the tuna steaks over direct heat for about 1-2 minutes per side.
10. Serve the tuna steaks hot with the topping of sauce.

Nutritional Value:

- Calories 468
- Total Fat 20.4 g

- Saturated Fat 4.2 g
- Cholesterol 83 mg
- Total Carbs 7.3 g
- Sugar 2 g

- Fiber 2.3 g
- Sodium 583 mg
- Potassium 769 mg
- Protein 52.1 g

Cod in Tomato Sauce

Preparation Time: 20 minutes
Cooking Time: 35 minutes
Servings: 5
Ingredients:

- 1 teaspoon dried dill weed
- 2 teaspoons sumac
- 2 teaspoons ground coriander
- 1½ teaspoons ground cumin
- 1 teaspoon ground turmeric
- 2 tablespoons olive oil
- 1 large sweet onion, chopped
- 8 garlic cloves, chopped
- 2 jalapeño peppers, chopped
- 5 medium tomatoes, chopped
- 3 tablespoons tomato paste
- 2 tablespoons fresh lime juice
- ½ cup water
- Salt and ground black pepper, as required
- 5 (6-ounce) cod fillets
- ½ cup fresh parsley, chopped

Method:

1. For spice mixture: in a small bowl, add the dill weed and spices and mix well.
2. In a large, deep skillet, heat the oil over medium-high heat and sauté the onion for about 2 minutes.
3. Add the garlic and jalapeno and sauté for about 2 minutes.
4. Stir in the tomatoes, tomato paste, lime juice, water, half of the spice mixture, salt and pepper and bring to a boil.
5. Reduce the heat to medium-low and cook, covered for about 10 minutes; stirring occasionally.
6. Meanwhile, season the cod fillets with the remaining spice mixture, salt and pepper evenly.
7. Place the fish fillets into the skillet and gently, press into the tomato mixture.

8. Increase the heat to medium-high and cook for about 2 minutes.
9. Reduce the heat to medium and cook, covered for about 10-15 minutes or until desired doneness of the fish.
10. Serve hot with the garnishing of the parsley.

Nutritional Value:

- Calories 285
- Total Fat 7.7 g
- Saturated Fat 1.2 g
- Cholesterol 94 mg
- Total Carbs 12.5 g

- Sugar 6 g
- Fiber 3.2 g
- Sodium 334 mg
- Potassium 947 mg
- Protein 41.4 g

Stuffed Swordfish

Preparation Time: 15 minutes

Cooking Time: 14 minutes

Servings: 2

Ingredients:

- 1 (8-ounce) (2-inch thick) swordfish steak
- 1½ tablespoons olive oil, divided
- 1 tablespoon fresh lemon juice
- 2 cups fresh spinach, torn into bite size pieces
- 1 garlic clove, minced
- ¼ cup feta cheese, crumbled

Method:

1. Preheat the outdoor grill to high heat. Lightly, grease the grill grate.
2. Carefully, cut a slit on one side of fish steak to create a pocket.
3. In a bowl, add 1 tablespoon of the oil and lemon juice and mix.
4. Coat the both sides of fish with oil mixture evenly.
5. In a small skillet, add the remaining oil and garlic over medium heat and cook until heated.
6. Add the spinach and cook for about 2-3 minutes or until wilted.
7. Remove from the heat.
8. Stuff the fish pocket with spinach, followed by the feta cheese.
9. Grill the fish pocket for about 8 minutes.
10. Flip and cook for about 5-6 minutes or until desired doneness of fish.
11. Cut the fish pocket into 2 equal sized pieces and serve.

Nutritional Value:

- Calories 296
- Total Fat 17 g
- Saturated Fat 5.5 g
- Cholesterol 73 mg
- Total Carbs 2.5 g
- Sugar 1.1 g
- Fiber 0.7 g
- Sodium 365 mg
- Potassium 613 mg
- Protein 32.5 g

Garlicky Shrimp

Preparation Time: 15 minutes
Cooking Time: 6 minutes
Servings: 4
Ingredients:

- 2 tablespoons olive oil
- 3 garlic cloves, sliced
- 1-pound shrimp, peeled and deveined
- 1 tablespoon fresh rosemary, chopped
- ½ teaspoon red pepper flakes, crushed
- Salt and ground black pepper, as required
- 1 tablespoon fresh lemon juice

Method:

1. In a large skillet, heat the oil over medium heat and sauté the garlic slices or about 2 minutes or until golden brown.
2. With a slotted spoon, transfer the garlic slices into a bowl.
3. In the same skillet, add the shrimp, rosemary, red pepper flakes. salt and black pepper and cook for about 3-4 minutes, stirring frequently.
4. Stir in the lemon juice and remove from the heat.
5. Serve hot with a topping of the garlic slices.

Nutritional Value:

- Calories 202
- Total Fat 9.1 g
- Saturated Fat 1.7 g
- Cholesterol 239 mg
- Total Carbs 3.2 g
- Sugar 0.1 g
- Fiber 0.5 g
- Sodium 317 mg
- Potassium 218 mg
- Protein 26.1 g

Mussels with Tomatoes & Wine

Preparation Time: 15 minutes
Cooking Time: 15 minutes
Servings: 6
Ingredients:

- 1 tablespoon olive oil
- 2 celery stalks, chopped
- 1 onion, chopped
- 4 garlic cloves, minced
- ½ teaspoon dried oregano, crushed
- 1 (15-ounce) can diced tomatoes
- 1 teaspoon honey
- 1 teaspoon red pepper flakes, crushed
- 2 pounds mussels, cleaned
- 2 cups white wine
- Salt and ground black pepper, as required
- ¼ cup fresh basil, chopped

Method:

1. In a large skillet, heat the oil over medium heat and sauté the celery, onion and garlic for about 5 minutes.
2. Add the tomato, honey and red pepper flakes and cook for about 10 minutes.
3. Meanwhile, in a large pan, add mussels and wine and bring to a boil.
4. Simmer, covered for about 10 minutes.
5. Transfer the mussel mixture into tomato mixture and stir to combine.
6. Season with salt and black pepper and remove from the heat.
7. Serve hot with the garnishing of basil.

Nutritional Value:

- Calories 244
- Total Fat 6 g
- Saturated Fat 1 g
- Cholesterol 473 mg
- Total Carbs 14.3 g
- Sugar 4.4 g
- Fiber 1.5 g
- Sodium 473 mg
- Potassium 791 mg
- Protein 19.1 g

Seafood Stew

Preparation Time: 20 minutes
Cooking Time: 25 minutes
Servings: 6
Ingredients:

- 2 tablespoons olive oil
- 1 medium onion, chopped finely
- 2 garlic cloves, minced
- ¼ teaspoon red pepper flakes, crushed
- ½ pound plum tomatoes, seeded and chopped
- 1/3 cup white wine
- 1 cup clam juice
- 1 tablespoon tomato paste
- Salt, as required
- 1-pound snapper fillets, cubed into 1-inch size
- 1-pound large shrimp, peeled and deveined
- ½ pound sea scallops
- 1/3 cup fresh parsley, minced
- 1 teaspoon fresh lemon zest, grated finely

Method:

1. In a large Dutch oven, heat oil over medium heat and sauté the onion for about 3-4 minutes.
2. Add the garlic and red pepper flakes and sauté for about 1 minute.
3. Add the tomatoes and cook for about 2 minutes.
4. Stir in the wine, clam juice, tomato paste and salt and bring to a boil.
5. Reduce the heat to low and simmer, covered for about 10 minutes.
6. Stir in the seafood and simmer, covered for about 6-8 minutes.
7. Stir in the parsley and remove from heat.
8. Serve hot with the garnishing of lemon zest.

Nutritional Value:

- Calories 313
- Total Fat 7.8 g
- Saturated Fat 1.1 g
- Cholesterol 207 mg
- Total Carbs 11.6 g
- Sugar 4.1 g

- Fiber 1.3 g
- Sodium 474 mg
- Potassium 455 mg
- Protein 44.3 g

Chapter 10: Meat & Poultry Recipes

Pistachio Lamb Chops

Preparation Time: 15 minutes
Cooking Time: 10 minutes
Servings: 4
Ingredients:
For Chops:

- ½ teaspoon ground cumin
- 1/8 teaspoon ground cinnamon
- Salt and ground black pepper, as required
- 8 (4-ounce) lamb loin chops, trimmed
- 1 tablespoon olive oil

For Pistachio Topping:

- 3 tablespoons pistachios, chopped finely
- 1 garlic clove, minced
- 2 teaspoons fresh lemon peel, grated finely
- 1½ tablespoons fresh cilantro, chopped
- 1½ tablespoons fresh parsley, chopped
- Salt, as required

Method:

1. In a large bowl, add the spices, salt and black pepper and mix well.
2. Add the lamb chops and coat with spice mixture generously.
3. In a large skillet, heat oil over medium-high heat and sear the chops for about 4-5 minutes per side or until desired doneness.
4. Meanwhile, for topping: in a bowl, mix together all ingredients.
5. Serve the chops with the topping of pistachio mixture.

Nutritional Value:

- Calories 470
- Total Fat 21.5 g
- Saturated Fat 6.6 g
- Cholesterol 204 mg

- Total Carbs 1.5 g
- Sugar 0.3 g
- Fiber 0.5 g

- Sodium 228 mg
- Potassium 810 mg
- Protein 64.4 g

Lamb Chops with Veggies

Preparation Time: 20 minutes
Cooking Time: 27 minutes
Servings: 4
Ingredients:

- 8 (4-ounce) lamb loin chops
- ½ cup fresh basil leaves
- ½ cup fresh mint leaves
- 1 tablespoon fresh rosemary leaves
- 2 garlic cloves
- 3 tablespoons olive oil
- 2 zucchinis, sliced
- 1 red bell pepper, seeded and cut into large chucks
- 1 eggplant, sliced
- 1¾ ounces feta cheese, crumbled
- 8 ounces cherry tomatoes

Method:

1. Preheat the oven to 390 degrees F.
2. In a food processor, add the fresh herbs, garlic and 2 tablespoons of the oil and pulse until smooth.
3. Transfer the herb mixture into a large bowl.
4. Add the lamb chops and coat with the herb mixture evenly.
5. Refrigerate to marinate for about 2-3 hours.
6. In the bottom of a large baking sheet, place the zucchini, bell pepper and eggplant slices and drizzle with the remaining oil.
7. Arrange the lamb chops on top in a single layer.
8. Bake for about 20 minutes.
9. Remove from the oven and transfer the chops onto a platter.
10. With a piece of foil, cover the chops to keep warm.
11. Now, place the cherry tomatoes into the baking sheet with veggies and top with the feta cheese.
12. Bake for about 5-7 minutes or until the cheese just starts to become golden brown.
13. Serve the chops alongside the vegetables.

Nutritional Value:

- Calories 619
- Total Fat 23.6 g
- Saturated Fat 9.4 g
- Cholesterol 215 mg
- Total Carbs 17.1 g

- Sugar 8.7 g
- Fiber 7.4 g
- Sodium 331 mg
- Potassium 1500 mg
- Protein 69.2 g

Leg of Lamb with Potatoes

Preparation Time: 20 minutes

Cooking Time: 1¼ hours

Servings: 8

Ingredients:

For Lamb & Potatoes:

- 1 (4-pound) bone in leg of lamb, fat trimmed
- Salt and ground black pepper, as required
- 5 garlic cloves, sliced
- 8 medium potatoes, peeled and cut into wedges
- 1 medium onion, peeled and cut into wedges
- 1 teaspoon garlic powder
- 1 teaspoon paprika
- 2 cups water

For Spice Mixture:

- ½ cup olive oil
- ¼ cup fresh lemon juice
- 5 garlic cloves, peeled
- 2 tablespoons dried mint
- 2 tablespoons dried oregano
- 1 tablespoon paprika
- ½ tablespoon ground nutmeg

Method:

1. Remove the leg of lamb from the refrigerator and set aside in room temperature for about 1 hour before cooking.
2. For spice mixture: in a food processor, add all the ingredients and pulse until smooth.
3. Transfer the spice mixture into a bowl and set aside.
4. Preheat the broiler of the oven.
5. With paper towels, pat dry the leg of lamb completely.
6. With a sharp knife, make a few slits on both sides the leg of lamb and season with salt and black pepper.
7. Place the leg of lamb onto a wire rack and arrange the rack onto the top oven rack.

8. Broil for about 5-7 minutes per side.
9. Remove from the oven and transfer the leg of lamb onto a platter to cool slightly.
10. Now, set the oven temperature to 375 degrees F. Arrange a rack in the middle of the oven. Place a wire rack into a large roasting pan.
11. Carefully, insert the garlic slices in the slits of leg of lamb and rub with spice mixture generously.
12. In a bowl, add the potato, onion, garlic powder, paprika and a little salt and toss to coat well.
13. Place 2 cups of water into the bottom of the prepared roasting pan
14. Place the leg of lamb in the middle of the prepared roasting pan and arrange the potato and onion wedges around the lamb.
15. With a large piece of foil, cover the roasting pan.
16. Roast for about 1 hour.
17. Remove the foil and roast for about 10-15 minutes more.
18. Remove from the oven and place the leg of lamb onto a cutting board for at least 20 minutes before carving.
19. Cut into desired sized slices and serve alongside potatoes.

Nutritional Value:

- Calories 700
- Total Fat 29.9 g
- Saturated Fat 8 g
- Cholesterol 204 mg
- Total Carbs 37.9 g
- Sugar 3.6 g
- Fiber 6.5 g
- Sodium 208 mg
- Potassium 1700 mg
- Protein 68.1 g

Lamb Shanks with Veggies

Preparation Time: 25 minutes
Cooking Time: 3 hours 25 minutes
Servings: 4
Ingredients:

- 1 tablespoon vegetable oil
- 4 (½-pound) lamb shanks
- 2 cups green olives, pitted
- 3 carrots, peeled and cut into ½-inch pieces
- 1 large celery root, peeled and cut into ½-inch pieces
- 1 large onion, minced
- 1 garlic clove, minced
- 2 tablespoons fresh ginger, grated
- 1 cup red wine
- 4 plum tomatoes, peeled, seeded and chopped
- 2 tablespoons lemon rind, grated
- 1 bay leaf
- ¼ teaspoon ground cinnamon
- ¼ teaspoon ground coriander
- ¼ teaspoon ground cumin
- ½ teaspoon red pepper flakes
- 3 cups low-sodium chicken broth
- Salt and ground black pepper, as required
- ¼ cup parsley leaves, minced
- ¼ cup cilantro leaves, minced

Method:

1. In a large, heavy-bottomed pan, heat the oil over medium heat and sear the shanks for about 5 minutes per side or until golden brown.
2. With a slotted spoon, transfer the shanks onto a plate and set aside.
3. In the same pan, add the olives, carrots, celery, onion, garlic and ginger over medium heat and cook for about 5 minutes, stirring frequently.
4. With a slotted spoon, transfer the vegetables onto a plate and set aside.

5. In the same pan, add the wine over high heat and cook for about 5 minutes, scraping up the brown bits
6. Add the shanks, vegetables, tomatoes, lemon rind, bay leaf and spices and stir to combine.
7. Reduce the heat to medium-low and simmer, covered partially for about 3 hours.
8. Stir I the salt and black pepper and remove from the heat.
9. Serve immediately with the garnishing of parsley and cilantro.

Nutritional Value:

- Calories 554
- Total Fat 24.9 g
- Saturated Fat 4.4 g
- Cholesterol 0 mg
- Total Carbs 35.5 g
- Sugar 16.5 g
- Fiber 10.9 g
- Sodium 900 mg
- Potassium 604 mg
- Protein 37.7 g

Ground Lamb Koftas

Preparation Time: 15 minutes

Cooking Time: 10 minutes

Servings: 6

Ingredients:

For Lamb Koftas:

- 1-pound ground lamb
- 2 tablespoons plain Greek yogurt
- 2 tablespoons onion, grated
- 2 teaspoons garlic, minced
- 2 tablespoons fresh cilantro, minced
- 1 teaspoon ground coriander
- 1 teaspoon ground cumin
- 1 teaspoon ground turmeric
- Salt and ground black pepper, as required
- 1 tablespoon olive oil

For Yogurt Sauce:

- ½ cup fat-free plain Greek yogurt
- ¼ cup roasted red bell pepper, chopped
- 2 teaspoons garlic, minced
- 1 teaspoon ground coriander
- 1 teaspoon ground cumin
- ½ teaspoon red pepper flakes, crushed
- Salt, as required

Method:

1. For Koftas: in a large bowl, add all the ingredients except lamb and mix until well combined.
2. Make 12 equal sized oblong patties.
3. In a large nonstick skillet, heat oil over medium-high heat and cook the patties for about 10 minutes or until browned completely, flipping occasionally
4. Meanwhile, for sauce: in a bowl, add all the ingredients and mix until well combined.
5. Serve the Koftas alongside the yogurt sauce.

Nutritional Value:

- Calories 189
- Total Fat 8.4 g
- Saturated Fat 2.6 g
- Cholesterol 70 mg
- Total Carbs 3.8 g
- Sugar 2.3 g
- Fiber 0.4 g
- Sodium 105 mg
- Potassium 361 mg
- Protein 23.1 g

Steak with Hummus

Preparation Time: 15 minutes
Cooking Time: 17 minutes
Servings: 6
Ingredients:

- ¼ cup fresh oregano leaves, chopped
- 1½ tablespoons garlic, minced
- 1 tablespoon fresh lemon peel, grated
- ½ teaspoon red pepper flakes, crushed
- Salt and ground black pepper, as required
- 1 pound (1-inch thick) boneless beef top sirloin steak
- 1½ cups prepared hummus
- 1/3 cup feta cheese, crumbled

Method:

1. Preheat the gas grill to medium heat. Lightly, grease the grill grate.
2. In a bowl, add the oregano, garlic, lemon peel, red pepper flakes, salt and black pepper and mix well.
3. Rub the garlic mixture onto the steak evenly.
4. Grill, covered for about 12-17 minutes, flipping occasionally.
5. Transfer the steak onto a cutting board for about 5 minutes.
6. With a sharp knife, cut the steak into desired sized slices.
7. Divide the steaks and hummus onto serving plates and serve with the topping of the feta cheese.

Nutritional Value:

- Calories 280
- Total Fat 12.8 g
- Saturated Fat 4 g
- Cholesterol 75 mg
- Total Carbs 12.2 g
- Sugar 0.6 g
- Fiber 5.2 g
- Sodium 408 mg
- Potassium 5117 mg
- Protein 29.6 g

Steak with Yogurt Sauce

Preparation Time: 15 minutes
Cooking Time: 15 minutes
Servings: 6
Ingredients:
For Steak:

- 3 garlic cloves, minced
- 2 tablespoons fresh rosemary, chopped
- Salt and ground black pepper, as required
- 2 pounds flank steak, trimmed

For Sauce:

- 1½ cups plain Greek yogurt
- 1 cucumber, peeled, seeded and chopped finely
- 1 cup fresh parsley, chopped
- 1 garlic clove, minced
- 1 teaspoon fresh lemon zest, grated finely
- 1/8 teaspoon cayenne pepper
- Salt and ground black pepper, as required

Method:

1. Preheat the grill to medium-high heat. Grease the grill grate.
2. For steak: in a large bowl, add all the ingredients except steak and mix well.
3. Add the steak and cost with mixture generously.
4. Set aside for about 15 minutes.
5. Grill the steak for about 12-15 minutes, flipping after every 3-4 minutes.
6. Transfer the steak onto a cutting board for about 5 minutes.
7. Meanwhile, for sauce: in a bowl, add all the ingredients and mix well.
8. With a sharp knife, cut the steak into desired sized slices and serve with the topping of the yogurt sauce.

Nutritional Value:

- Calories 354
- Total Fat 13.7 g
- Saturated Fat 5.9 g
- Cholesterol 87 mg
- Total Carbs 8.1 g
- Sugar 5.3 g
- Fiber 1.1 g
- Sodium 162 mg

- Potassium 802 mg
- Protein 46.3 g

Beef & Tapioca Stew

Preparation Time: 20 minutes
Cooking Time: 1¾ hours
Servings: 8
Ingredients:

- 1 tablespoon olive oil
- 2 pounds boneless beef chuck roast, cut into ¾-inch cubes
- 1 (14½-ounce) can diced tomatoes with juice
- ¼ cup quick-cooking tapioca
- 1 tablespoon honey
- 2 teaspoons ground cinnamon
- ¼ teaspoon garlic powder
- Ground black pepper, as required
- ¼ cup red wine vinegar
- 2 cups beef broth
- 3 cups sweet potato, peeled and cubed
- 2 medium onions, cut into thin wedges
- 2 cups prunes, pitted

Method:

1. In a Dutch oven, heat 1 tablespoon of oil over medium-high heat and sear the beef cubes in 2 batches for bout 4-5 minutes or until browned.
2. Drain off the grease from the pan.
3. Stir in the tomatoes, tapioca, honey, cinnamon, garlic powder, black pepper, vinegar and broth and bring to a boil.
4. Reduce the heat to low and simmer, covered for about 1 hour, stirring occasionally.
5. Stir in the onions and sweet potato and simmer, covered for about 20-30 minutes.
6. Stir in the prunes and cook for about 3-5 minutes.
7. Serve hot.

Nutritional Value:

- Calories 675
- Total Fat34. 1 g
- Saturated Fat 13 g
- Cholesterol 117 mg
- Total Carbs 59.6 g
- Sugar 26 g
- Fiber 7.1 g
- Sodium 295 mg

- Potassium 1150 mg
- Protein 34.1 g

Beef, Artichoke & Mushroom Stew

Preparation Time: 20 minutes
Cooking Time: 2¼ hours
Servings: 6
Ingredients:
For Beef Marinade:

- 1 onion, chopped
- 1 garlic clove, crushed
- 2 tablespoons fresh thyme, hopped
- ½ cup dry red wine
- 2 tablespoons tomato puree
- 2 tablespoons olive oil
- 1 teaspoon cayenne pepper
- Pinch of salt and ground black pepper
- 1½ pounds beef stew meat, cut into large chunks

For Stew:

- 2 tablespoons olive oil
- 2 tablespoons all-purpose flour
- ½ cup water
- ½ cup dry red wine
- 12 ounces jar artichoke hearts, drained and cut into small chunks
- 4 ounces button mushrooms, sliced
- Salt and ground black pepper, as required

Method:

1. For marinade: in a large bowl, add all the ingredients except the beef and mix well.
2. Add the beef and coat with the marinade generously.
3. Refrigerate to marinate overnight.
4. Remove the beef from bowl, reserving the marinade.
5. In a large pan, heat the oil and sear the beef in 2 batches for about 5 minutes or until browned.
6. With a slotted spoon, transfer the beef into a bowl.
7. In the same pan, add the reserved marinade, flour, water and wine and stir to combine.

8. Stir in the cooked beef and bring to a boil.
9. Reduce the heat to low and simmer, covered for about 2 hours, stirring occasionally.
10. Stir in the artichoke hearts and mushrooms and simmer for about 30 minutes.
11. Stir in the salt and black pepper and bring to a boil over high heat.
12. Remove from the eat ad serve hot.

Nutritional Value:

- Calories 367
- Total Fat 16.6 g
- Saturated Fat 4 g
- Cholesterol 101 mg
- Total Carbs 9.6 g
- Sugar 2.2 g
- Fiber 3.1 g
- Sodium 292 mg
- Potassium 624 mg
- Protein 36.7 g

Chicken, Dried Fruit & Olives Casserole

Preparation Time: 20 minutes
Cooking Time: 50 minutes
Servings: 4
Ingredients:

- 6 ounces dried apricots, quartered
- 6 ounces dried prunes, quartered
- 4 ounces green olives, pitted
- 2 ounces capers
- 2 garlic cloves, crushed
- 2 tablespoons fresh oregano, minced
- Salt and ground black pepper, as required
- 1 bay leaf
- 2/3 cup red wine vinegar
- ¼ cup olive oil
- 4 (6-ounce) chicken breasts
- 3 tablespoons brown sugar
- ¾ cup white wine

Method:

1. For marinade: in a large baking dish, add the apricots, prunes, olives, capers, garlic, oregano, salt, black pepper, bay leaf, vinegar and oil and mix until well combined.
2. Add the chicken breasts and coat with the marinade generously.
3. Refrigerate, covered overnight.
4. Remove from the refrigerator and set aside in the room temperature for at least 1 hour before cooking.
5. Preheat the oven to 325 degrees F.
6. Remove the chicken breasts from the bowl and arrange in a baking dish in a single layer.
7. Spread the marinade over the chicken breasts evenly and sprinkle with the brown sugar.
8. Place the white wine around the chicken breasts.
9. Bake for about 50 minutes.
10. Serve the chicken breasts with the topping of pan sauce.

Nutritional Value:

- Calories 559
- Total Fat 22.5 g
- Saturated Fat 4.6 g
- Cholesterol 99 mg
- Total Carbs 44.4 g
- Sugar 27.3 g
- Fiber 6.2 g
- Sodium 775 mg
- Potassium 555 mg
- Protein 40.4 g

Grilled Chicken Breasts

Preparation Time: 15 minutes
Cooking Time: 12 minutes
Servings: 4
Ingredients:

- 4 (4-ounce) boneless, skinless chicken breast halves
- 3 garlic cloves, chopped finely
- 3 tablespoons fresh parsley, chopped
- 3 tablespoons olive oil
- 3 tablespoons lemon juice
- 1 teaspoon paprika
- ½ teaspoon dried oregano
- Salt and ground black pepper, as required

Method:

1. With a fork, pierce chicken breasts several times
2. In a large bowl, add all the ingredients except the chicken breasts and mix until well combined.
3. Add the chicken breasts and coat with the marinade generously.
4. Refrigerate to marinate for about 2-3 hours.
5. Preheat the grill to medium-high heat. Grease the grill grate.
6. Remove chicken from marinade and grill for about 5-6 minutes per side.
7. Serve hot.

Nutritional Value:

- Calories3 15
- Total Fat 19.1
- Saturated Fat 3.9 g
- Cholesterol 101 mg
- Total Carbs 1.6 g
- Sugar 0.3 g
- Fiber 0.5 g
- Sodium 141 mg
- Potassium 330 mg
- Protein 33.2 g

Chicken & Veggie Kabobs

Preparation Time: 20 minutes
Cooking Time: 10 minutes
Servings: 8
Ingredients:

- ¼ cup white vinegar
- ¼ cup fresh lemon juice
- ¼ cup olive oil
- 2 garlic cloves, minced
- ½ teaspoon dried thyme, crushed
- ½ teaspoon dried oregano, crushed
- 1 teaspoon ground cumin
- Salt and ground black pepper, as required
- 2 pounds skinless, boneless chicken breast, cubed into ½-inch size
- 1 large orange bell pepper, seeded and cubed into 1-inch size
- 1 large green bell pepper, seeded and cubed into 1-inch size
- 16 fresh mushrooms
- 16 cherry tomatoes
- 1 large red onion, quartered and separated into pieces

Method:

1. In a large bowl, add the vinegar, lemon juice, oil, garlic, dried herbs, cumin, salt and black pepper and mix until well combined.
2. Add the chicken cubes and coat with mixture generously.
3. Refrigerate, covered to marinate for about 2-4 hours.
4. Preheat the outdoor grill to medium-high heat. Grease the grill grate.
5. Remove the chicken from the bowl and discard the excess marinade.
6. Thread the chicken and vegetables onto pre-soaked wooden skewers respectively.
7. Grill for about 10 minutes, flipping occasionally or until desired doneness.
8. Serve hot.

Nutritional Value:

- Calories 232
- Total Fat 10.7 g
- Saturated Fat 2.5 g
- Cholesterol 66 mg
- Total Carbs 7.1 g
- Sugar 4 g

- Fiber 1.7 g
- Sodium 68 mg

- Potassium 298 mg
- Protein 27.4 g

Chicken with Caper Sauce

Preparation Time: 20 minutes
Cooking Time: 18 minutes
Servings: 5
Ingredients:
For Chicken:

- 2 eggs
- Salt and ground black pepper, as required
- 1 cup dry breadcrumbs
- 2 tablespoons olive oil
- 1½ pounds skinless, boneless chicken breast halves, pounded into ¾-inch thickness and cut into pieces

For Capers Sauce:

- 3 tablespoons capers
- ½ cup dry white wine
- 3 tablespoons fresh lemon juice
- Salt and ground black pepper, as required
- 2 tablespoons fresh parsley, chopped

Method:

1. For chicken: in a shallow dish, add the eggs, salt and black pepper and beat until well combined.
2. In another shallow dish, place breadcrumbs.
3. Dip the chicken pieces in egg mixture then coat with the breadcrumbs evenly.
4. Shake off the excess breadcrumbs.
5. In a large skillet, heat the oil over medium heat and cook the chicken pieces for about 5-7 minutes per side or until desired doneness.
6. With a slotted spoon, transfer the chicken pieces onto a paper towel-lined plate.
7. With a piece of the foil, cover the chicken pieces to keep them warm.
8. In the same skillet, add all the sauce ingredients except parsley and cook for about 2-3 minutes, stirring continuously.
9. Stir in the parsley and remove from heat.
10. Serve the chicken pieces with the topping of capers sauce.

Nutritional Value:

- Calories 352
- Total Fat 13.5 g
- Saturated Fat 3.5 g
- Cholesterol 144 mg
- Total Carbs 16.9 g

- Sugar 1.9 g
- Fiber 1.2 g
- Sodium 419 mg
- Potassium 111 mg
- Protein 35.7 g

Chapter 11: Dessert Recipes

Frozen Strawberry Yogurt

Preparation Time: 15 minutes
Servings: 16
Ingredients:

- 3 cups plain Greek yogurt
- 1 cup sugar
- ¼ cup fresh lemon juice
- 2 teaspoons pure vanilla extract
- Pinch of salt
- 1 cup fresh strawberries, hulled and sliced
- ¼ cup fresh mint leaves

Method:

1. In a bowl, add all the ingredients except the strawberries and beat until smooth.
2. Transfer the yogurt mixture into an ice cream maker and process according to the manufacturer's directions, adding the strawberry slices in the last minute.
3. Now, transfer the mixture into an airtight container and freeze for about 3-4 hours.
4. Remove from the freezer and set aside at room temperature for about 10-15 minutes before serving.
5. Serve with the garnishing of mint leaves.

Nutritional Value:

- Calories 86
- Total Fat 0.6 g
- Saturated Fat 0.5 g
- Cholesterol 3 mg
- Total Carbs 16.7 g
- Sugar 16.3 g
- Fiber 0.3 g
- Sodium 45 mg
- Potassium 133 mg
- Protein 2.8 g

Pistachio Ice-Cream

Preparation Time: 15 minutes
Cooking Time: 15 minutes
Servings: 6
Ingredients:

- 2 cups whole milk
- 1 cup unsalted pistachios, finely ground
- ¾ cup sugar, divided
- ½ teaspoon vanilla extract
- 5 egg yolks
- ½ cup whole pistachios
- 1½ cups heavy cream

Method:

1. In a pan, add all the milk, ground pistachios and ¼ cup of the sugar and bring to a boil, stirring frequently.
2. Stir in the vanilla extract and remove from the heat.
3. In a bowl, add the remaining sugar and egg yolks and beat well.
4. With a ladle, add some hot milk, stirring continuously until well combined.
5. Add the egg yolk mixture into the pan and mix well.
6. Place the pan over medium-low heat and cook for about 7-10 minutes, stirring frequently.
7. Remove from the heat and through a strainer, strain the mixture into a bowl.
8. Refrigerate the bowl for about 2 hours.
9. Remove from the refrigerator and stir in the heavy cream and whole pistachios.
10. Transfer the mixture into an ice cream maker and process according to the manufacturer's directions.
11. Now, transfer the mixture into an airtight container and freeze for about 2 hours before serving.

Nutritional Value:

- Calories 372
- Total Fat 24.5 g
- Saturated Fat 10.5 g
- Cholesterol 224 mg
- Total Carbs 34.1 g
- Sugar 30.4 g
- Fiber 1.5 g
- Sodium 131 mg

- Potassium 310 mg
- Protein 8.5 g

Roasted Pears

Preparation Time: 15 minutes
Cooking Time: 25 minutes
Servings: 6
Ingredients:

- ¼ cup pear nectar
- 3 tablespoons honey
- 2 tablespoons butter, melted
- 1 teaspoon fresh orange zest, grated
- 3 ripe medium Bosc pears, peeled and cored
- ½ cup mascarpone cheese
- 2 tablespoons powdered sugar
- 1/3 cup salted pistachios, chopped

Method:

1. Preheat the oven to 400 degrees F.
2. In a bowl, add the pear nectar, honey, butter and orange zest and mix well.
3. In a 2-quart rectangular baking dish, arrange the pears, cut sides down and top with the honey mixture.
4. Roast for about 20-25 minutes, spooning liquid over pears occasionally.
5. Remove from the oven and transfer the pears onto serving plates with some of the cooking liquid.
6. In a bowl, add the mascarpone cheese and powdered sugar and mix well.
7. Top the pears with the cheese mixture and serve with the garnishing of pistachios.

Nutritional Value:

- Calories 215
- Total Fat 9.6 g
- Saturated Fat 4.5 g
- Cholesterol 21 mg
- Total Carbs 31.4 g
- Sugar 23.5 g
- Fiber 4 g
- Sodium 73 mg
- Potassium 219 mg
- Protein 4.1 g

Fruity Yogurt Parfait

Preparation Time: 20 minutes
Cooking Time: 10 minutes
Servings: 4
Ingredients:

- 2 cups plain Greek yogurt
- ¼ cup honey
- ¼ cup water
- 2 tablespoons sugar
- ½ teaspoon fresh lime zest, grated finely
- ¼ teaspoon ground cinnamon
- ¼ teaspoon vanilla extract
- 2 peaches, pitted and quartered
- 4 plums, pitted and quartered
- ¼ cup almonds, toasted and chopped

Method:

1. In a bowl, add the yogurt and honey and mix until well combined.
2. Set aside.
3. In a pan, mix together the remaining ingredients except the almonds over medium heat and cook for about 8-10 minutes or until fruits becomes tender, stirring occasionally.
4. Remove from the heat and set aside at room temperature to cool.
5. Divide half of the yogurt mixture into 4 tall serving glasses evenly.
6. Divide the fruit mixture over yogurt evenly and top each with the remaining yogurt.
7. Garnish with almonds and serve.

Nutritional Value:

- Calories 269
- Total Fat 4.9 g
- Saturated Fat 1.5 g
- Cholesterol 7 mg
- Total Carbs 48.5 g
- Sugar 46.3 g
- Fiber 2.9 g
- Sodium 87 mg
- Potassium 589 mg
- Protein 9.5 g

Chocolate Mousse

Preparation Time: 15 minutes

Cooking Time: 5 minutes

Servings: 4

Ingredients:

- 3½ ounces dark chocolate, chopped
- ¾ cup milk
- 1 tablespoon honey
- ½ teaspoon vanilla extract
- 2 cups plain Greek yogurt
- 2 tablespoons fresh raspberries
- 1 tablespoon chocolate shaving

Method:

1. In a pan, add the chocolate and milk over medium-low heat and cook for about 3-5 minutes or until chocolate melts, stirring continuously.
2. Add the honey and vanilla extract and stir to combine well.
3. Remove from the heat and set aside at room temperature to cool slightly.
4. In a large glass bowl, place the yogurt and chocolate mixture and gently, stir to combine.
5. Refrigerate to chill for about 2 hours.
6. Serve with the topping of the raspberries and chocolate shaving.

Nutritional Value:

- Calories 262
- Total Fat 9.8 g
- Saturated Fat 7 g
- Cholesterol 17 mg
- Total Carbs 30.5 g
- Sugar 28 g
- Fiber 1.1 g
- Sodium 127 mg
- Potassium 415 mg
- Protein 10.5 g

Baklava

Preparation Time: 20 minutes
Cooking Time: 50 minutes
Servings: 18
Ingredients:

- 1-pound nuts (pistachios, almonds, walnuts), chopped
- 1 teaspoon ground cinnamon
- 1 (16-ounce) package phyllo dough
- 1 cup butter, melted
- 1 cup white sugar
- 1 cup water
- ½ cup honey
- 1 teaspoon vanilla extract

Method:

1. Preheat the oven to 350 degrees F. Grease a 9x13-inch baking dish.
2. In a bowl, add the nuts and cinnamon and toss to coat well.
3. Set aside.
4. Unroll the phyllo dough and cut in half.
5. Arrange 2 dough sheets into the prepared baking dish and coat with some butter.
6. Repeat with 8 dough sheets in layers and sprinkle with 2-3 tablespoons of nut mixture.
7. Repeat with remaining dough sheets, butter and nuts.
8. With a sharp knife, cut into diamond shapes all the way to the bottom of the baking dish.
9. Bake for about 50 minutes or until top becomes golden and crisp.
10. Meanwhile, for sauce: in a pan, add the sugar and water and cook until sugar is melted, stirring continuously.
11. Stir in the honey and vanilla extract and simmer for about 20 minutes.
12. Remove the baklava from oven and immediately place the sauce on top evenly.
13. Set aside to cool before serving.

Nutritional Value:

- Calories 435
- Total Fat 27.8 g
- Saturated Fat 9.7 g
- Cholesterol 31 mg

- Total Carbs 43.5 g
- Sugar 22.6 g
- Fiber 3.2 g

- Sodium 409 mg
- Potassium 200 mg
- Protein 7.1 g

Tahini Cookies

Preparation Time: 20 minutes
Cooking Time: 15 minutes
Servings: 30
Ingredients:

- 1½ cups whole-wheat pastry flour
- 1 tablespoon baking soda
- Pinch of salt
- ¾ cup sugar
- ½ cup butter, softened
- ½ cup tahini
- 1 tablespoon orange blossom water
- 1 tablespoon honey
- 1 medium egg

Method:

1. In a large bowl, mix together the flour, baking soda and salt.
2. In the bowl of a stand mixer, add the sugar and butter and beat on medium-high speed until light and fluffy.
3. Add the tahini and beat well.
4. Add the orange blossom water and honey and beat until well combined.
5. Add the egg and beat on low speed until well combined.
6. Slowly, add the flour mixture, mixing well until a dough form.
7. With a plastic wrap, cover the bowl and refrigerate for about 1 hour.
8. Preheat the oven to 350 degrees F. Line 2 baking sheets with parchment paper.
9. With 2 tablespoons of dough, make balls and arrange onto the prepared baking sheets about 3-inch apart.
10. With the back of a lightly, floured fork, gently flatten each ball.
11. Bake for about 13-15 minutes or until golden brown.
12. Remove from the oven and place the baking sheets onto the wire racks for about 5 minutes.
13. Carefully, invert the cookies onto the wire racks to cool completely before serving.

Nutritional Value:

- Calories 97
- Total Fat 5.4 g

- Saturated Fat 2.3 g
- Cholesterol 14 mg
- Total Carbs 11.2 g
- Sugar 5.6 g
- Fiber 0.5 g
- Sodium 158 mg
- Potassium 27 mg
- Protein 1.5 g

Conclusion

The Mediterranean diet is based upon the cuisines and culture of the Mediterranean region. Numerous scientific and medical studies have argued and proven that the Mediterranean diet is very healthy and is a perfect diet plan for avoiding various chronic diseases like cancer, cardiac complications and also for boosting life expectancy. The Mediterranean diet is very different in its fat intake from the rest of the diet plans. Mediterranean cuisine involves higher content of unsaturated fat like olive oil and lower content of saturated fats. Saturated fats are mainly present in dairy products and meat apart from their slight presence in a few nuts, avocados and certain vegetable oils. Numerous well-known scientific studies claim that the risk of heart-related complications and diseases can be lowered by increasing the intake of a type of dietary fat i.e. the mono-saturated fat, which is present mostly in olive oils. This argument of studies has concluded that unsaturated fats have been credited with a high amount of HDL cholesterol which is also referred to as "the good" cholesterol. The reason for HDL cholesterol being credited as a friend for the body is that protects the body from cardiovascular complications.

Made in the USA
San Bernardino, CA
03 November 2019